STOP!

WHAT ARE YOU WAITING FOR?

YOUR STEP-BY-STEP GUIDE TO ESTATE PLANNING

YVETTE E. TAYLOR-HACHOOSE

Second Wind Press

WASHINGTON CROSSING, PENNSYLVANIA

Published by
Second Wind Press
P.O. Box 407
Washington Crossing, Pennsylvania 18977

Cover photograph by Stephen Hudgins

For information about special discounts for bulk purchases, please place order at www.ythlaw.com

ISBN 0-9653942-3-9

Library of Congress Catalog Card Number: 2009901575

To my sister Deborah T. Salahu-Din

She has always encouraged me to write, especially with passion about what matters most in my life and work. Her extraordinary literary expression appeared when she was a young child and unfolded, as the petals of a perfect rose, over the ensuing years. I am eternally grateful for her talent and depth of knowledge as well as her support of this writing endeavor that will help to make a difference for generations.

ABOUT THE AUTHOR

Yvette E. Taylor-Hachoose of the Law Offices of Yvette E. Taylor-Hachoose is a 1982 graduate of Georgetown University Law Center. She has 27 years of legal experience including corporate law department experience as a Vice President of Prudential Insurance Company and as Assistant General Counsel for CIGNA Corporation and Prudential Insurance Company. In private practice since 2004 at her offices in Washington Crossing and Philadelphia, Pennsylvania, she represents families, individuals, and businesses in a wide range of legal matters including estate planning, asset protection planning, business succession planning, wills, trusts, living wills, powers of attorney, probate, mediation, elder law and guardianships. Ms. Taylor-Hachoose regularly lectures to professional and lay audiences on the subject matter of this book. You can blog with her at www.buckscountyattorney.blogspot.com for up-to-date estate planning information.

ACKNOWLEDGMENTS

Writing this book has been a labor of love, and there are so many people to thank as I think about those along the way who urged me on, provided feedback, listened to my ideas, and shared their wisdom.

I have received one of the most tremendous blessings in my family. My parents Edward and Doretta Taylor instilled in me the importance of believing in myself and my goals. They have taught me this by letting me become the person that I am, never interfering but always guiding, supporting, and being positive examples. To all of my family, Richard, Diana and Angelina Hachoose; Deborah Salahu-Din, Derrick, Janna and Mikayla Amin; Tyrone, Amy, Donovan and Briana Taylor; and my extended family which includes a host of aunts, uncles, and cousins, without your support this goal in my life would not be possible.

In my practice, I have wonderful clients who encouraged me to share more of what I do to as many as I can reach. This is my attempt to fulfill their wish. I am so thankful to my paralegal Christine Barta for inputting the first very rough draft into the computer and believing in the vision.

To the audiences that I have spoken before, I thank you for your insight. Your questions are answered in this book. I especially thank one of my first audiences at a meeting for the Association of the Blind. Their questions were extensive and probing. They challenged me to simplify complex concepts.

To Carole Stovall, Pamela Bridgewater, Russell Arawkard, Veronica Landon, Richard Newman, Tahiya Nyahuma, Mujahid Nyahuma, Dorothy Foster, Carl Utter, Marcia Hartman, Andy Smith, Frederica Gaffney, Allison Young, Medenia Dashiell, Norma Cobbs, Justin Barta, and my many friends and colleagues for being in the right place at the right time when I needed some inspiration or direction. I thank you all.

CONTENTS

PART 1: If Not Now, When? If Not You, Who?

PART 2: You Can't Take It With You

PART 3: The Journey of Your Estate

PART 4: Giving and Living Longer

LETTER TO READER

Dear Reader:

The fact that you have purchased *this* book, my book, is a really good step toward understanding estate planning. There are certainly many books that have been written about estate planning, and although you may have perused some of them, you most likely have not taken all the necessary action to plan your estate adequately. So I ask you to stop procrastinating *now*. What are you waiting for? Each one of you will have different reasons that you have not acted or have acted half-heartedly. So at this moment I ask you to use my concise, handy, and uncomplicated step-by-step guide to estate planning, which I believe will spur you to the action you want and need to take. This guide makes estate planning simple, understandable, relevant, obtainable, immediate, enlightening, clear, calming, and useful. It provides you with the steps to get your important affairs in order *now, and now* is the time to take an inventory of your life's work and worth. My book will help you accomplish that goal!

I have written this volume for you to read ideally from cover to cover to maximize the contents and impact. However, you can read chapters out of sequence as the topics interest you or address your unique needs, and return to other chapters later. No matter which approach you choose, I assure you that you'll get the essential estate planning themes because throughout the book I revisit, repeat, and emphasize important points for you to remember.

In Chapter 1 I introduce hypothetical scenarios describing individuals and family situations which undoubtedly may have something in common with your own experiences or with someone you know. You will see these individuals reappear throughout the book as their circumstances change, just like your own circumstances will change over time. This is to help you understand clearly how to apply a particular estate planning method or procedure which may otherwise be confusing.

1

So dear reader, please sit down now and read this book with the promise to yourself that when you are "leaving it all behind," you'll have planned for your family and friends with peace of mind. You and your family will be glad you did!

Yvette E. Taylor-Hachoose
2009

ESTATE PLANNING LESSONS
FROM
MICHAEL JACKSON'S DEATH

On Thursday, June 25, 2009, as this manuscript was being ushered into publication, Michael Jackson, born August 29, 1958, died at age 50. The shock of his death was felt around the world, for he was revered as the King of Pop. So many people grew up on his music and experienced each phase of his musical genius, from the Jackson 5 debut when he was just five years old to his dynamic solo career. His music evolved and gathered new fans throughout four decades.

Michael Jackson's death further underscores the reason that I speak and write about the essentials of estate planning. I remind my audiences that you can only plan when you are living!!! **What lessons can we learn from the estate planning done by Michael Jackson?** Five lessons that have arisen thus far are addressed in my book, and I am certain many more will arise during what is the beginning of a long and complex estate planning saga.

First, you must have a will that is up-to-date and valid. **Second**, you must name the guardian of your minor children and address potential issues and challenges from a surviving parent who is not named as guardian. **Third**, you must name the executors who will gather up and protect your assets and ensure distribution in accordance with your will. **Fourth**, you must provide for the distribution of your assets, but you are not required to provide for parents, siblings, an ex-wife, or other family members. **Fifth**, unlike a will, a trust, with all its terms and conditions, is not a public document.

One editor of my book recently commented that as a result of reading my manuscript, she clearly understood the issues being reported about Michael Jackson's estate planning affairs. It is my ardent plea that you not only read this book but that you take the necessary action now to plan your estate while you are still living.

Yvette E. Taylor-Hachoose
July 17, 2009

FOREWORD

Y ou might ask, "What is estate planning and why a book about it?" Estate planning can be accurately described as a planning process that entails the preparation of legal documents necessary to protect your health and property during life and at death. The most common components of an estate plan include wills, trusts, and powers of attorney. Estate planning covers you and people associated with you and the problems they face at your death. Spouses, children, grandchildren, dependents, business partners and others will suffer not only emotionally but economically if you fail to plan. Taking care of the human element, people issues, is a primary objective of estate planning. Because you care about your loved ones, your health, and/or your property, you need an estate plan.

Why a book about estate planning? It will help you understand the process involved and walk you through it using concrete examples that illustrate the process. With that information, you can take the next step towards planning your own estate. Therefore, a book about estate planning that addresses the myriad of examples for its application will help you see how estate planning applies to your specific situation.

I have found that there are three broad views that most people have when asked about estate planning and its application to their circumstances. First, there is the traditional view that estate planning only involves passing on money or real estate after death or determining guardianship of minor children. For example, estate planning may be for the graduate student who has an inheritance (money) to manage; the doctor who has acres of vacation properties that sit on the Marcellus Shale, ripe for gas exploration and potentially oil to consider; or, the corporate executive who has young adopted children to nurture and support. However, understand that estate planning is not just about money, real estate, and guardianship.

There is the expanded view of estate planning that addresses non-traditional assets. Such estate planning is for individuals who, during their lifetime, cultivate their human potential into valuable assets to pass on to others. Estate planning, in such cases, may be for the retired school teacher who has the handwritten manuscript, spanning over three decades, of his book on the Korean War; the soccer Mom who has a summer camp for kids; or, the artist who has music royalties and copyrights. Without advance planning now, these individuals' legacies could be lost forever.

A third view may not be a view at all but an untapped potential resource for an expanded category of individuals who also need to engage in the estate planning process. I read about a two-year study by William Marsten, a prominent psychologist, who asked 3,000 people the following question: "What have you to live for?" He discovered that amazingly 94% of those interviewed had no definite purpose. For me, that means that those individuals did not realize the importance of their own traditional assets nor the potential of their nontraditional assets or their legacy. The men and women interviewed and many more like them are not active participants in their own lives. They are in a holding pattern, like a plane on a runway awaiting clearance to take off. But, what clearance are they all waiting for? How will they ascertain their life's purpose so they too can soar?

If this study is indicative of our society, most of us are not living life. We are merely enduring life or letting life just happen to us. I have come to realize that if we contemplate our life circumstances now, we will discover our purpose and what we may have to pass on. Starting my estate planning law practice allowed me, for the first time, to really understand life and how to be an active participant every moment. Writing this book is my way to share my purpose, which is to help make a difference now and for future generations. The estate planning process requires that you assess your life now, to identify your assets (traditional or nontraditional), to determine your beneficiaries (family or otherwise), and to control when and how your assets are distributed.

Estate planning provides you with a way of addressing your needs while you are living and developing a plan that expands beyond your lifetime. This book will answer many questions that you have regarding estate planning. What is estate planning? How do you implement an effective estate plan? When do you begin the process of estate planning? More importantly, this book will challenge you to reflect on your life. You can engage the estate planning process as a process of self-discovery to help you understand the life that you are living. It may be the first time that you plant an idea of your purpose that can begin to germinate into your legacy. It is never too late! You are worth it! So, what are you waiting for?

PREFACE

Just imagine a beautiful spring day in the nation's capital amidst the cherry blossoms. The mayor of the city of Tokyo presented the cherry trees to the city of Washington in 1912. It was an offering of friendship that the United States reciprocated with a gift of flowering dogwood trees to the people of Japan. When floods destroyed cherry trees in Japan, cuttings from the original gift served to restore the presence of the blooming splendor of the cherry trees. This cycle of giving therefore came full circle when the trees again fulfilled their role as a symbol and agent of friendship.

I reflect back now on this single, simple gesture that has spawned over ten decades of remembrance celebrations. The annual Cherry Blossom Festival and activities commemorate what has now become a momentous, historic, and nationally recognized event. I take pause, for I am always in awe of the power of a single action. An informed and thoughtful act can lead to an expanding and perpetual resource, blossoming for many generations. And that is how I see the role of estate planning in the lives of my clients.

This book has been several years in the making. However, its seed was planted in the early 1980's in Washington, D.C. where I studied decedents' estates (property left when a person dies) at Georgetown University Law Center. Since then, I have marveled at the ability of some families to create a dynasty from limited beginnings and of other families to squander a fortune in one generation. I realized then that the haves and have nots were not permanent status. I learned, and later in my law practice perfected, the essential tools for preserving, protecting, and distributing an individual's estate.

The art of estate planning is not a mystery and is accessible to all who seek it. It serves as the process of creating an informed and well executed plan that can lead to an expanding and long-lasting resource, benefitting many generations. Taking an action now is the first step towards what can be of significance for generations. If you understand the significance of estate planning or if you do not, reading this book will help you advance your journey toward generational prosperity. The truth, therefore, is you will impact not only your own destiny but also the destiny of your children and other beneficiaries.

As I began writing this book, I realized that most people are still under the impression that they have no "estate." They think that "estate" only refers to massive fortunes created and preserved for generations. Therefore, a basic question that arises for many people is why is estate planning important to me? The question I posed back to them is how did it all begin? How were these massive fortunes created and preserved? "Old money," as it may be called, was amassed over long periods of time, but it all started during one person's lifetime. Throughout your lifetime, you too create a legacy worth preserving.

For example, in your personal life, your children form a part of your legacy. One of the most important things listed in parenting magazines for couples starting a family is having a will prepared, one designating guardianship of your minor children. When I was surveying people for this book on potential questions to address, the question that was indeed prevalent was, "Who should serve as guardian of my minor children?" There is no set answer to that question if the usual prospects are not available. Some couples have no living parents or have elderly parents. Still others have neither siblings nor friends to consider. However, you still are the only person who can best answer that question based on your family circumstances.

The case of Anna Nicole Smith illustrates the importance of determining guardianship in a current will. Former Playboy model celebrity Anna Nicole Smith (Vicki Lynn Marshall) died in 2007 at age thirty-nine, leaving a five month old baby, naming no father, and having an obsolete will that left everything to a deceased son and omitted provisions for future born children. Even after paternity was determined, the litigation and law commentaries continued over other unresolved questions. My advice is to take the time now to survey the list of potential guardians for your minor children, make a decision regarding guardianship, and stay current by updating your will when necessary. In fact, the lesson to be learned from this case is the importance of a properly drafted estate plan in order to protect your children who are an essential part of your legacy.

Even if you do not have children, you have other loved ones, a home, other real estate, personal property, including artwork, jewelry and collectibles and yes, pets. You have charitable interests as well as intangible experiences and life lessons to document for the benefit of future generations. Think about the stories you have heard about some elderly people who have worked and saved their money leaving a small fortune at their death. Without a will, this money, saved over a lifetime, could be wasted on undeserving heirs. With a will, the money could be used to educate a generation of scholars or be used to establish a permanent facility for the health and well-being of a community.

In your business life, you may have a company. Planning is important to assure that you preserve those assets so the business will continue to provide the needed products or services and continue to be an income source for your family.

If you do not have your estate plan in order, the legacy you intended to leave your loved ones may experience these outcomes:

1. The wrong relatives or other undeserving individuals may inherit your property.

2. Significant amounts of money and time may be wasted in court litigating over your assets as well as over the guardians of minor children.

3. Your family personal business could become public spectacle in open court or the media.

4. Loved ones could inherit property outright and at a young age and perhaps squander their inheritance because they lack the maturity, knowledge, and guidance to protect their inheritance.

5. An inheritance may not be protected from mismanagement, creditors, divorce proceedings, and bankruptcy court.

It is very common for people to spend thousands of dollars on things like plasma TVs, computer systems, music systems, cameras, cars, boats, and trips but nothing to protect their families and loved ones if they were to die unexpectantly.

Do not let that happen to you. Begin the process now. You can start with a simple will. You can advance from a basic trust to a complex trust addressing tax planning and asset protection. You can establish a family partnership or family or public foundation. You can make sure you appoint people whom you want to oversee your assets and your health if you are disabled or incapacitated. With planning, taking a single, simple action step now, you too can spawn decades of remembrance celebrations, family and community festivities that commemorate your momentous and historic action for the benefit of your loved ones.

Part 1:

**IF NOT NOW, WHEN?
IF NOT YOU, WHO?**

1: Benefits of Estate Planning

The essential parts of this book evolved from a series of educational seminars I developed and conducted, *Everything You Wanted to Know About Estate Planning But Did Not Know to Ask*. Since the preparation of the initial materials and power point presentations, I have conducted extensive research in preparing this book and perfected the contents into what is now a comprehensive reference guide for the consumer and the professional advisor. By following my advice, you will become an educated consumer equipped to obtain the best possible professional guidance in accomplishing your estate planning goals.

What Are the Benefits of Estate Planning?

Sometimes we can see the importance of something through the experiences of others. In this first chapter, I will introduce individuals in hypothetical situations that may resonant with you and develop them in succeeding chapters. Through these examples, I want to encourage, motivate, and inspire you to prepare for your future and the security of your family for generations to come. This comprehensive guide to preserving your wealth will detail the seven essential benefits of estate planning, which are protecting assets, saving money, creating a legacy, distributing wealth, addressing special circumstances, insuring peace of mind and discerning needs as you age. Using the knowledge you acquire from reading this guide will advance you on your journey to generational prosperity.

1. **Protects Assets**

Eve and Bob both inherited wealth and made a lot more money beyond their inheritance. They now breed show dogs and actively participate in charities benefiting animals. They only have one daughter, Julia, who at thirty-six still can not quite make it on her own. She has already experienced personal bankruptcy and, given her unemployment history, would be on welfare if not for her parents' continued support. They want to make sure Julia will not become destitute when they die. Therefore, instead of leaving money outright to her upon their death, their estate plan includes a trust for the money left for Julia, who is not fiscally responsible enough to manage the money herself. A trust is effective because Eve and Bob appointed a trustee to both manage and distribute the money for Julia's benefit.

The cash left for Julia by her parents will not be subject to the claims of Julia's creditors. Nor will the cash be subject to any further bankruptcy, lawsuits, or divorce settlement Julia may experience in the future. It is Eve's and Bob's legacy that is being protected. They have the right to determine who will be the recipient of their bounty.

There is no one way of defining assets. In other words, assets can be defined in many different ways. For Eve and Bob, money represents their primary asset. How do you define your assets? Do you consider your children, your home, or the money you have accumulated over your lifetime, as Eve and Bob did, your assets? Do you consider yourself an asset? However you define assets, it is important to know that we all have assets, and they are worth protecting.

2. **Saves Money**

Max and Margaret have high-level corporate careers at companies where they now hold highly appreciated stock options. Both of them have personal passions. For over 30 years, Max has collected historical manuscripts and other memorabilia on the American Revolution. Margaret formed a local foundation that supports women and girls in her local community. She also has a fine art collection that rivals the collection of her local museum. Their three sons (two of which are sons from Max's first marriage) are married with children and have their own successful businesses. The federal estate tax consequences would be significant (almost ½ of their estate would be at risk) if Max and Margaret did not engage in any estate planning. Further, if they reside in a state with inheritance tax, planning could avoid costly mistakes. Clearly, they do not want money they have accumulated over their lifetime to be depleted by taxes and other circumstances that, with advance planning, they can control.

Through effective estate planning, Max and Margaret can reduce or eliminate their federal estate tax. Throughout your lifetime you, like Max and Margaret, have accumulated wealth in one form or another. Under the current federal estate tax law, individuals have an available tax credit against the ultimate estate tax due. This tax credit is a direct dollar-for-dollar reduction of an individual's tax liability, compared with tax deduction, which reduces an individual's tax liability only in proportion to his or her tax bracket. Therefore, for married couples, each has a tax credit against the ultimate estate tax. However, the estate tax is not due, for married couples, until the second spouse dies. This is because property left to a spouse is tax free. The first spouse to die would transfer his or her estate to the surviving spouse free of an estate tax. It is not until the death of the second spouse that the entire estate is subject to estate tax. At that time, the tax credit of the second spouse to die would be available to offset the amount of estate tax due. With advance planning, the tax credit available to the first spouse to die can be preserved and would then be available at the death of the second spouse to further reduce the estate tax due.

Max and Margaret would both (since we do not know who may die first – though the statistic indicates that wives outlive their husbands) need to have a specific trust set up to shelter or preserve the applicable tax credit of the lifetime exclusion. The lifetime exclusion is the amount (value of an individual's estate) that is not subject to federal estate tax. In 2009, that amount is 3.5 million dollars. The tax savings of this amount passes to the three sons of Max and Margaret upon the death of the second spouse. The tax credit of the second spouse to die will also pass tax free to the sons. As a result, seven million dollars would effectively be saved from taxes through the single, simple act of estate planning.

Max and Margaret can also save on state inheritance tax. Who will get Margaret's extensive art collection? If she leaves it to a charitable organization or qualified non-profit, there would be no taxes. However, her sons may also have an interest in art. In order to avoid the taxes on personal property, Margaret could begin gifting during her lifetime some of her art collection to her sons. There would be no taxes if she is under her one million dollar lifetime exclusion amount for gifting.

All of this requires planning on the part of Max and Margaret. In the long term as well as the short term, the value of a little planning today goes a long way to your family's future savings and security.

3. **Creates a Legacy**

What about Max's historical memorabilia on the American Revolution? How can he preserve this passion for the historical significance of a major event in American history? Through estate planning, he can build upon this legacy. Future generations could benefit from the knowledge these documents provide. Max can even make sure the next generation is guided by his wisdom by giving specific instructions on the use of assets. He does not want to lose the momentum of his collection through ineffective management by his sons if their interests should differ. Professional advice and guidance now can make the difference between creating a legacy and losing an accumulated treasure of the past.

Max's legacy can be addressed in many ways. If he wants to leave assets to his sons but their interests or passions differ from his, then he can leave the collection in a trust. He can fund the trust and choose a trustee who will be responsible for preserving the assets he accumulated in a way that he may designate. If his interest is charitable, he can give in a number of ways to those who will cherish his generosity, including institutions of higher education, museums, or organizations of scholarly pursuit. Estate planning can even enable Max to create a legacy of philanthropy that can include the involvement of his sons and grandchildren. This book will cover the options and alternatives available to Max and others similarly situated.

4. <u>Distributes Wealth</u>

Ria enjoys the international travel required of her successful technology consulting business. During her extensive traveling and demanding business, her closest and dearest sibling Michele has taken on the full responsibility of the care of their parents, whose health has been rapidly failing. Her two older brothers have remained distant from the family and provide no support or interest in the care of their parents. Though Ria never married, she is considering adopting children. In recent times, Ria has thought about her estate and how it might be distributed when she dies. She is especially concerned about the ramification of any adoption.

Should the state control the distribution of Ria's assets? If she does not take any action, the state will control the distribution of her assets. Under the intestate laws (applicable when you die without a will) of some states, her parents would inherit her entire estate since she does not have a husband or any children presently. However, with her parent's failing health, this may not be the wisest option for Ria. She would probably want to leave some assets for their care but upon their death, control where their assets, if any, would be distributed. She could do this with proper planning. If Ria's parents predeceased her, Ria's estate would be equally distributed to her older siblings Michele and her two brothers. Though Ria's brothers are her heirs, she can decide, with estate planning, who inherits and who does not inherit her wealth. She controls whether assets are distributed at once or over an extended time period and for specific reasons, i.e. for the care of her parents. It is her choice, her decision, her plan.

There is something to be said about creating a plan that gives you control of the distribution of assets accumulated through your ingenuity and labor. An estate plan would allow Ria to designate the guardian of her minor children if she were to adopt. It would allow her to appoint her own executors and trustees to administer her estate in accordance with her directive. If she does not address these and other important issues affecting her assets, the state will.

No one wants to leave to the state the important decisions of who gets their assets and who administers their estate. It is within everyone's power to take control and plan now.

5. Addresses Special Circumstances

Linwood and Jordan lived together for ten years before they adopted their special needs son Julian, who was 10 years old at the time of the adoption. Julian has thrived and progressed significantly over the last sixteen years with the love, attention, and hard work of his parents, one of whom is a nurse. Julian's Seeing Eye dogs have helped, and his current dog is an integral part of his life. All of this has enabled Julian to live on his own with the support of state programs.

We all have some special circumstances in our lives. Linwood and Jordan are not married and have no contact with their families. They will have to address their property interests through advance planning, which would be inclusive of a will and other estate planning documents. This type of planning is even more important given the special needs of Julian. When either or both of his parents die, what happens to Julian? How would his public benefits be affected if money were left directly, and not in a trust, to Julian? Through estate planning, his parents can supplement and not disrupt the programs working to provide Julian an independent life.

Your special and unique circumstances can and should be covered appropriately. You can take the initiative to assure this is done to your satisfaction through estate planning.

6. Ensures Peace of Mind

With the recent loss of his wife, Jack is now rearing three young children on his own. As an only child, he can not rely on any help from his mother Mary or his father Charles. Mary is still working beyond her retirement years just to be able to take care of herself and her husband. Charles has been diagnosed with a mentally debilitating form of Alzheimer's, which the doctors do advise could be hereditary. As the sole person responsible for his children, Jack wants to have peace of mind when it comes to their future. Therefore, he has made several inquiries into estate planning to get that peace of mind. He wants to make sure his children are taken care of when he dies. If he does not take the necessary steps to address guardianship of his children upon his death, then he leaves them in unnecessary turmoil and additional pain.

Choosing a guardian for minor children is a major decision. It is a decision that takes careful consideration. Without planning, Jack burdens Mary with making decisions he failed to address in advance. Even more tragic, imagine leaving questions of guardianship to the state or court with no firsthand knowledge of Jack's children's gifts, talents, needs, and desires. Only Jack can choose the best guardian for his children.

Families unfortunately can fall apart over unaddressed estate planning. Estate planning gives you peace of mind now and will be appreciated by those you leave behind.

7. Discerns Elder Needs

In 2006, the oldest of the baby boomers, the generation born between 1946 and 1964, turned 60 years old. As a result, new concerns have given rise to the specialized area of "elder law." This term was not even mentioned when I attended law school in the early 1980's. However, with the anticipated increase in the elderly population, the advances in technology, and the increase in life expectancy, the dynamics of our society are changing and the elder law area of practice is growing rapidly. Elder law looks at the needs of seniors, like Mary and Charles, during their longer lifetime. Estate planning, as well as retirement and long-term care planning, forms a natural part of the elder law practice. Seniors, like Mary, are finding themselves working longer to address the cost of healthcare for elders under their care. In Mary's case, it is her husband, but it could very well have been her parents. Mary and Charles are not unusual in their circumstances given our aging society.

It is also important for those like Jack, who are still young and working to think and plan early for their longer lifetime. Jack realizes that he has to be concerned about the potential hereditary aspect of his father's illness. Jack may need someone to handle his financial affairs if he becomes incapacitated or disabled. The same applies for his healthcare matters. If his physicians are unable to communicate with him, who does he want them to turn to for answers? This is especially important when considering end-of-life illnesses and life-support preferences. Does Jack want to be kept on life-support if he is determined to be in a vegetative state? Those are hard decisions that should not be left to people he has not designated. The fact that we are living longer requires all of us to take a real careful look at long term care questions and put plans in place.

Given the seven benefits of estate planning, why have most people failed to engage in estate planning? I have found that once people understand the benefits of estate planning, they have another question that must be addressed: "How do you implement an effective estate plan?" That is an important question, and there is no short answer. In fact, it is this question that generated my interest in writing this book because the answer takes a whole book. The detailed answer to the question can be found in the chapters that follow. However, in this chapter, I will provide a brief response to the question and expand upon it in remaining chapters.

How Do You Implement an Effective Estate Plan?

There are specific essential documents used in the estate planning process. These documents not only take effect at the time of death but also are applicable during your lifetime. As you age, you have so many reasons to take necessary planning steps. If you become incompetent, you can no longer engage in estate planning on your own behalf. It is at this time that the courts may become involved. A determination of guardianship by the court is very costly. You save time and you save money when you plan now.

The first and most important document that everyone should have is a will. Unfortunately, most people do not have a will, and those who do, have not updated it, even though their circumstances have changed in ways that require an updated will.

Another important document in the estate planning process is the general power of attorney. It is used to appoint an agent to handle business affairs if you are unable. Generally, this occurs as a result of your incapacity.

A third essential document is the healthcare power of attorney. With this document, you appoint an agent to address healthcare issues when your doctor or healthcare professional is unable to communicate with you. It also provides your agent with the authority to have access to your medical records.

The fourth basic document in the estate planning process is the living will. This is also known as an advanced directive for healthcare. It allows you to state your preference regarding life support when you have a terminal or end-stage condition. This would include a permanent vegetative state or other end-of-life condition where recovery is not possible.

The will, general power of attorney, healthcare power of attorney, and living will are the essential documents required in any estate plan. They lay the foundation for the more advanced estate planning techniques elaborated upon further in this book.

When Do You Begin to Plan Your Estate?

Once people know the seven benefits of estate planning and how to implement an effective plan, the third and final question asked is when is estate planning done? The simple answer is now.

If you are eighteen or older and of sound mind, then you can and should have, at a minimum, a will. Many people use certain triggering events to start their estate plan. This would include events like buying a house, getting married, having a child, or developing a particular passion.

Now is as good a time as any to begin with estate planning for the first time. Now is also a good time to review your estate plan. In fact, periodic reviews should be established at the time that your initial estate plan is done. There may be a change in your circumstances that affect your estate plan, or the laws may have changed since you executed your estate plan. Why wait putting off until tomorrow what you can and should do now? Procrastination in estate planning is not beneficial to you or your family.

Since your estate plan is a part of your life plan, these documents are created during your lifetime and can be changed. For example, a will can be amended by a codicil, a modification to your existing will, or it can be totally changed by revoking the will and making another one. All prior documents should be shredded and discarded once new documents are executed. Any copies or originals given to other people should be retrieved, shredded, and discarded as well.

Everyone has an estate. An estate encompasses all of your assets which are all the things acquired during your lifetime. If you have children, it also covers children and those whom you want to be responsible for your minor children. A child's loss of a parent is traumatic enough. When both parents die and the child is a minor, it really gives you reason to pause and hope that this potentiality was already addressed by the parents. Why should family members have to fight over the care of a minor child or, worse yet, be unwilling to take on the responsibility? When you prepare a will, you can determine who is or who is not willing or capable of serving as the guardian of your minor children. Your children should not be in the middle at such a critical time. They are your most precious resource, and your advanced planning for them will be invaluable.

In addition to your things and your children, as part of your estate plan, you want to preserve your interest and your passions. Given all of these aspects of estate planning, an estate plan can be plain and simple. It can be as complex as you want or as your estate may require. Working with a knowledgeable professional can help make even the most complex situations manageable for you. So there is never a need to stay away from estate planning for concern of simplicity or fear of complexities. In either case, professionals can serve you the best.

If you should fail to engage in any advance planning, all your assets are subject to the distribution plans of the state where you reside. The state's plan is governed by the intestate laws. These laws control the distribution of the estate if you die without a will. These laws are not made with your specific situation in mind and, therefore, do not address all family needs. In fact, the intestate laws do not keep up with your changing family dynamics, and these laws unfortunately can leave out important people in your life. In order to avoid, as much as possible, disputes among family members or litigation which will result in diminishing assets, it is best to have your own plan in place.

In the final analysis, estate planning now is an opportunity. It is your opportunity to override the state's plan for your assets. It is your opportunity to reflect with excitement and pleasure on your life, your accomplishments, and your interests. It is your opportunity to come up with a plan that represents your intentions. In fact, the process of estate planning is one of the most important ventures for your family.

2: Coordination of the Estate Planning Process

The primary objective of estate planning is taking care of the people you love. In order to accomplish this task, the coordination of your estate planning team, your asset distribution, and your fiduciary selection are required. Further, a thorough review of your financial and personal circumstances with your estate planning team helps to address the preservation and protection of your estate by ultimately eliminating or reducing potential tax exposure as well as keeping your assets out of the reach of creditors. Through estate planning you address the distribution of your estate by controlling who inherits and when they inherit. When you are ready to do an estate plan, the issue that needs to be addressed is how to proceed.

Reflecting on one of the hypothetical situations in Chapter One, imagine Eve and Bob are relaxing at home one quiet evening. The telephone rings. Eve glances at the caller ID.

"It's Julia calling from her cell phone," Eve announces to Bob as she picks up the phone. The call from their daughter proceeds as follows for Bob as he listens and wonders what new drama is about to unfold. Of course he is only privy to Eve's part of the conversation.

"Hi, honey. How are you?"

"Well, tell me what happened?"

"Where is he now?"

"Yes, of course you can stay here."

"You don't have to ever go back to him if you don't want to dear."

"I know this is the second time. Don't worry, you left your first fiancée, you can leave your second one as well. I've always said you should never marry unless you are absolutely certain."

"Look, Julia, if you never get married, it will not be the end of the world."

"Now, just calm down, you are only 36, anything is possible."

"You did what? You quit your job just because he works there too."

"Yes, our money for your wedding is in the bank. Why? What do you want to do with the money?"

"Oh!!"

"Oh!!"

"Uhm!!"

"That's interesting!!"

"See you tomorrow."

Eve hangs up the phone and just stares at it for a moment. Realizing his wife expects him to say something, Bob turns toward Eve with a look of bewilderment. Eve calmly says to Bob, "We either plan now or our daughter will be destitute the moment we die."

Eve and Bob soon begin to coordinate their estate planning team. Starting and completing the estate planning process is one of the best things that they can do for Julia. Knowing just how the process works is what they need to know to begin.

Coordination of Your Team

Estate planning requires a team approach. Addressing estate planning matters can be confusing for many people. It is therefore comforting to know that your financial, business, and personal affairs can be coordinated during this estate planning process. This happens because the estate planning team members will generally be comprised of your attorney, financial advisor, insurance agent, and accountant. All are working together for your best interest.

Your estate planning attorney can serve as the coordinator of that team. If you choose an attorney to coordinate your team, you want someone who is experienced in the field of estate planning, an attorney with specific expertise in this ever-changing area of law.

Whether you choose an attorney to coordinate or lead your team or not, you want someone who is accessible and accountable to you. Estate planning is a very personal affair and so personal attention is essential.

When selecting an attorney, you want an attorney who has an affiliation with groups or organizations in the forefront of this area of practice and who stays current by attending continuing education classes, conferences, and seminars relevant to estate planning. If the attorney writes articles or books about estate planning or serves as a presenter or organizer of conferences, seminars or presentations, then you benefit from one who not only knows estate planning but also can explain it well to others.

At the first meeting, in addition to getting to know your estate planning attorney and understanding the process and everyone's role in the process, you begin to provide specific information regarding your assets. You need to have available for review any previously executed estate planning documents. Tax returns may also be helpful. If you can compile a list of your assets prior to the meeting, then do so. However, most of this information can be ascertained during the first meeting, and additional asset information can be provided later throughout the estate planning process. The information gathered at the first meeting helps to determine potential state inheritance tax, if your state has an inheritance tax, and potential federal estate tax exposure and how best to plan to minimize or eliminate the tax.

The questions posed during the first meeting will help you think through the issues that need to be addressed and how you may want these issues handled. This meeting is also the time for you to raise questions. You want to know the fee arrangements and clearly understand the basis of the fees. This is generally shared at the first meeting and confirmed in writing after your discussion.

As previously indicated, in addition to an attorney, the other essential team members include your financial advisor, insurance agent, and accountant. Each serves as the key to your estate planning success. It is important that you also meet with each member of your team to establish expectations. This is the most effective way to also determine their ability to meet your estate planning needs and the degree of trust and confidence you can place in each of them. Just like a doctor can instill confidence in a patient prior to surgery, your team should make you feel your life's assets are in the hands of professionals who care and know how to handle your particular estate planning situation. Your meeting can be held separately or jointly with each team member. Your team members could contact each other on an as needed basis. Your situation will dictate what is most appropriate for you.

When modifying your estate plan, your old documents should be shared with your attorney if the attorney is different from the one who prepared the documents. It is important to discuss the changes you want. But it is just as important for the attorney to review the old documents to assure everything is being distributed appropriately. Once the documents are completed, it is important that you review them and ask any questions that may further advance the planning process. You also want to review for accuracy prior to signing and, where required, notarizing. Afterward, shred the old documents because having more than one will or other estate planning documents could be problematic and confusing and could create family disharmony.

Coordination of Your Asset Distribution

The estate planning process requires the coordination of a team in order to assure the coordination of the distribution of your assets. Not all assets go through probate, the legal process of proving the terms, conditions, and existence of a will. Probate addresses the assets passed under the will. However, assets can be passed by beneficiary designation, through joint ownership and under a trust. Your financial advisor and your insurance agent can address any changes needed to beneficiary designations under your investment products and under insurance policies as part of your estate plan. Your accountant and your attorney can address the tax implication for the different methods of asset distribution upon death.

The coordination of the distribution of your assets is critical. It reflects how you want to distribute your assets to family members. For example, it may be your intent to treat all children equally. Therefore, you want to make sure that the life insurance beneficiary designation form lists all children, including children born after a policy may have been obtained. All beneficiary designation forms should be reviewed during the estate planning process. Revision should be consistent with your intent and desire. Any change in beneficiary designation should only occur once your estate planning documents are executed. This is particularly important if you are designating your estate as beneficiary.

You also want to coordinate any joint ownership with the overall intent of your estate plan. For example, many people may add the name of a child to their bank account for ease of handling bills and other payments. However, upon your death, at least half, if not more, of those funds would become the property of the child whose name appears on the account. The funds pass to the joint owner on the bank account. The funds would not pass under your will or go through the probate process. If it were your intent for the children to share equally in your estate, then you have to address the joint ownership. This could be done by reducing that child's interest under the will based upon their interest in the joint account. However, that may be difficult to ascertain. Another option would be to take your child's name off of the account and provide him or her with a General Power of Attorney to handle your financial affairs. The assets in the bank account would then pass under the terms of the will.

It is important to note that in the estate planning process, husband and wife can and generally are represented by the same attorney. After meeting with you, the attorney can advise you on whether there are any concerns that would preclude joint representation. The information between attorney and client is privileged and confidential and therefore can not be shared with any other person. However, as relates to joint representation, information provided by one spouse can not be withheld from the other spouse. All information must be shared. If conflicts should arise impacting the joint representation, then the attorney must cease representation and advise the couple to obtain separate counsel. For the most part, when couples are engaging in estate planning, their interests are not in conflict and an attorney routinely represents husband and wife without incident or problem. In fact, joint representation does help to maximize savings and preserve assets best for husband and wife.

Coordination of Your Fiduciaries

One of the most crucial decisions that you need to make early on in the estate planning process is who will be your fiduciaries, the persons who would be under a legal obligation to look out for your best interest. Your fiduciaries make sure that your estate is handled in accordance with your instructions and intentions. These instructions and intentions are for a specific purpose, which is to provide for your beneficiaries, those who will benefit from your estate.

Fiduciaries would include guardians, executors, trustees, and agents. The individual or individuals chosen are persons you trust who are able and willing to accept the responsibility of a fiduciary. Other things to consider as you choose your fiduciaries are whether the individuals have knowledge of your personal affairs or your personal preferences on important matters. Generally, these would be individuals to whom you are close and who know you well. They are not required to have any special training or expertise as long as they can be trusted and have the capacity to address the circumstances that may be presented to them. They can and often will seek out professional help to address matters that may not be in their area of expertise. This is a standard practice and is done in your best interest. However, one of the most important things that you can do is to advise those whom you may choose as fiduciary of your specific interests. The more information that you can provide up front to them, the less complex their role may be when they have to serve.

Corporate fiduciaries are also an important consideration. Just as when you choose an individual fiduciary, you want a corporate fiduciary that is trustworthy, capable, and willing to accept the role as fiduciary. During the estate planning process, you can research your corporate fiduciary options. The larger your estate, the more you have a need for an institutional fiduciary that will be around for a long period of time and that has the capability and capacity to address the complexities of a larger estate.

Choosing your fiduciaries is a significant accomplishment in estate planning. With the right fiduciaries in place, whether individuals or corporate or a combination thereof, you are well on the way to assuring that your overall estate planning goals are achieved.

Other Considerations

Keeping Your Estate Plan Current

It is important to understand that once you complete an estate plan, you must keep it current. The plan should be reviewed every three to five years. As a general rule, (everyone's situation is different), if you are between the ages of 18 and 55, every three years will be adequate. These ages represent the most active period for moving to other states, getting married, getting a divorce, having children, building wealth and assets, or having an inheritance left to you. As your life circumstances change over time, your estate plan should, where applicable, reflect such changes. If you are older than 55, every five years is sufficient because people generally experience less fluctuation in their lives as they grow older. During this period, the concerns shift to aging, disabilities, and long-term care, which are the elder law issues addressed in Chapter 14. However, regardless of age, if there has been any major change in your life circumstances or in the law, your estate plan should be reviewed at that time. Estate planning, therefore, is not a one time event. It is ongoing and consistently evolving, reflecting changes in your life circumstances and changes in laws that may impact your estate plan.

Document Execution and Location

Estate planning documents have no legal effect whatsoever until they are signed and, where required, notarized. Once you have reviewed and finalized the documents, you should proceed to have them executed immediately. As important as this may be, I have found on more than one occasion that people have held documents for years without having them executed. I remember one couple wanted to know if they should execute documents drafted more than three years prior. There are some people who never get around to executing documents prepared for them. That is why it is important that the attorney, or whomever you choose as the coordinator of your estate planning, should always make it a part of their practice to arrange the execution of all estate planning documents.

Once your estate planning documents are executed, you have several options for places to maintain your original documents. You can keep them in a safe deposit box at your bank or financial institution or a safe that is fireproof and waterproof in your home. The attorney can maintain your original documents for you as well. In many states like Pennsylvania, you do not have to file or register your will upon execution. It is only filed or registered at death.

It is your preference regarding the maintenance of your original documents. You also want to make sure those who will be serving in a fiduciary capacity know where your documents are located and can get to them when needed for your benefit.

Taxes

One of the important reasons to have an estate plan is to save on taxes. Tax planning is essential to make sure that your estate is not depleted over time by taxes. The primary taxes that have to be addressed at death are the state's inheritance tax, if any, and federal estate tax. The federal estate tax only applies if your estate is above the federal exemption amount that may be applicable at the time of death. There is no exemption amount for a state's (like Pennsylvania's) inheritance tax to apply. In Pennsylvania, the inheritance is taxed on the first dollar inherited. Therefore, for Pennsylvania, you want to know that the tax rate on assets left to a spouse or charity is 0%; for children the rate is 4.5%; for siblings the rate is 12%; and for all others the rate is 15%.

Beneficiaries

A beneficiary is someone whom you determine will benefit from the assets of your estate. Generally, beneficiaries are family members or other loved ones. It could even be a family pet.

Charities also serve as beneficiaries under many wills. A charity can represent a particular interest or passion that you may have during your lifetime. Giving to the charity can represent your way of continuing to fulfill your specific interest. There are many ways to implement charitable giving as more fully discussed in Chapter 13.

Attorney Fees

Legal fees are important to understand when hiring your attorney. In estate planning, many attorneys have different fee structures. The fee structure should be explained to you before you commit to engaging any legal services. The different options for fee structure include a flat fee for the services or documents requested, an hourly rate for the services provided or documents to be drafted, or a combination of flat fee for some documents and hourly rate for others. You should be advised whether any estimate or quote provided will change. This can happen if additional services, not initially contemplated, become necessary.

Many people think that estate planning will be expensive and therefore do not initiate a plan. However, it is more expensive when you do not act. With effective estate planning, you can save on state and federal taxes and you can protect assets from creditors. It also represents your plan for distribution of your assets and not the state's plan. The state's asset distribution plan (intestate law) is not focused upon saving you money or protecting your assets from potential creditors.

Part 2:

YOU CAN'T TAKE IT WITH YOU

3: Wills

I have entitled this section, *You Can't Take it With You.* However, this clearly was not the thinking of certain periods of the ancient Egyptian culture. For those with high social status, their wealth and treasures were entombed with them.

I have an interest in Egyptology, and over the years have collected replicas of treasures found in the tombs of Egyptian rulers. In my travel to Egypt, I visited museums and the ruins of the temples of many Egyptian pharaohs. The treasures found in the pharaohs' tombs have been well documented. There is probably no group of artifacts in the world more famous than those associated with the discovery of King Tutankhamun's tomb. The collection, which includes furniture, sculptures, and jewelry of gold, bronze, and ivory, has traveled the world.

I sometimes think about this ancient view of taking wealth and treasure literally to one's grave. I compare it with our modern western view of life after death. In our society, we do not entomb our possessions because we do not believe we will need them in the "afterlife," for those who believe in an "afterlife." But if we do not take them with us, what becomes of them? This question lies at the heart of what I do today, encouraging people to plan for the distribution of their worldly possessions to others. I view it as our way of assuring prosperity beyond our mortal lives.

What Makes a Will Legal?

As we build our estate plan, the will sits as its cornerstone. It is one of the most essential documents of your estate plan. However, most people do not have a will nor any other thought-out plan for distribution of their assets. Unlike in ancient Egyptian culture, you can't take your assets to your grave. As a result, without a will or some other planned distribution, issues are left unresolved and made more complicated. What is important to remember is the will is your testament expressing your last wishes. Like the celebrations of the pharaohs who planned elaborately for taking their assets "with them", making your will is your party. Look at the estate planning process as your opportunity to be as creative as you want. Have some fun with the process. Enjoy it. When you look forward to getting your will done, there is one less thing to worry about.

In most states, the legal requirements for a will are simple. You can execute a will if you are eighteen years old or older and of sound mind. The document can be typed or handwritten and must be signed at the end of the document. In states like Pennsylvania, you are not required to sign the document in front of witnesses. However, the practice is to have at least two witnesses present at the execution of the will. They also sign the document. This formality helps to ensure the will withstands possible challenge.

The wording in the will should be clear and unambiguous. Though you can freely write your will, it is wise to work with an estate planning attorney or other professional who can make sure your intent is clear and not subject to unwanted interpretations. If there are special terms used, those terms should be defined. It is also important to use legal names so that it is clear who is entitled to your wealth. The amount of time it takes to be very precise with your wording is time well spent.

You can choose to videotape the will signing ceremony, but you still have to satisfy the basic requirements of a valid will. Generally, videotaping is done to document the signing and to show that the person knew exactly what he or she was doing when the will was executed. You can further personalize the execution of the will with comments to family members. Therefore, the videotape can serve to eliminate a challenge if shared with the person who intends to dispute the validity of the will based upon the capacity of the person making the will.

There are other formalities that can be implemented. Though not required, your will can be notarized. Therefore, the witnesses to the will do not have to be located at your death to prove that the will is your document. The will becomes self-proving when notarized. In essence, notarizing validates the will as your document. The extra step of having your will notarized can avoid costly disputes down the road. If there is a potential for a dispute, this step is essential. Even if this is not the case, the nominal cost associated with having the document notarized makes it a basic step worth taking.

As an important practice, you should only have one original will and it should be kept in a safe place. The options include a waterproof and fireproof safe at your home, a safety deposit box at your bank, or a secure place with your attorney. If something happens to the original will while you are alive, then make another one which revokes all prior wills. It avoids confusion if the initial will is ever found. If you want to change your will, the original will must be shredded or destroyed to also avoid confusion.

It is the original that must be produced for probate. There is a presumption that if the original can not be found, that the individual who made the will revoked it by destroying the original. Therefore, if there is only a copy of the will available, it is difficult to overcome the presumption that it was revoked. This could result in a significant delay in probate. So take the necessary precautions to safeguard the original.

One final consideration when making a will is the use of a memorandum. As a separate document from your will, the memorandum can be placed with the will. It serves to delineate specifically those who are entitled to your specific pieces of personal property. This would include such things as jewelry, clothing, furniture, rugs, pictures, books, silver, linen, china, crystal, and art. It is used when you have a list of specific items that you want to distribute to a list of specific individuals. Since you may be acquiring additional personal property items at anytime, you do not want to have to change your will each time. The memorandum can be updated without any legal formalities. It is not a legally binding document, but it can serve as a helpful guidance to your executor. The memorandum is only an option to consider. Otherwise, the same information can be provided in the will, and any change would be subject to the legal formalities for changing the will.

What Are the Essential Roles of a Will?

One role of a will is to appoint your own executor. The executor is the person or institution who will be responsible for the administration of your estate. They make sure distribution is in accordance with your expressed wishes. They also have the responsibility to make sure that state inheritance tax returns and federal estate tax returns are filed. A person who serves as an executor can and, in many cases, is also a beneficiary under the will. With the exception of reimbursement for expenses, the executor is generally not compensated when he or she is also a beneficiary under the will. A reasonable compensation can be established for an individual serving as an executor who is not also a beneficiary. If you name an institution as your executor, your estate will be subject to the institution's applicable fee schedule. If the assets in your estate are significant, you could negotiate a fee arrangement with the institution in advance for the benefit of your estate.

A second role of your will is appointing a guardian for your minor children. Naming the guardian of your minor children is one of the most important tasks for a parent. You should not assume that there will be agreement among family members on this issue if you have not made a specific appointment. In fact, your appointment helps alleviate the involvement of the state or court in choosing the guardian of your children. Parents have asked me during the estate planning process who should they name. Even though they realize the importance of their decision, it is not clear in their mind who to appoint. I have only provided guidance based upon what has worked well for others. In that regard, for younger couples the parents of one spouse generally serve as the guardians. Also, appointing a responsible adult sibling is another viable choice if the grandparents are much older. However, if you are considering a couple as guardians, I would suggest that only one person of the couple be named in the will. It would be the person that you would want your children to be with if the couple divorces. That way your child does not become part of a custody battle. Therefore, in your will, you name only one person as the guardian realizing that as long as they are married, both would be providing the care of your minor children.

In the first chapter, I introduce Ria. She is seeking estate planning advice after adopting her son. In her case, she wants her sister Michele to serve as guardian. Ria's parents are in ill health, and her brothers have not been a part of her life since their childhood. However, if Ria dies before her parents, it may be difficult for Michele to serve as guardian because she is the primary care giver for her parents. It would be wise for Ria to name an alternate guardian if Michele, as primary guardian, is unable or unavailable to serve. A discussion with any potential guardian is critical so that the person can assess their life's circumstances and make a commitment of this magnitude.

A third role of the will is to provide a plan of distribution of your assets at death. The will allows you to distribute your assets to those you wish to share in your estate. Your assets include your money, home, timeshare, furniture, car, boat, jewelry, and collectibles. The distribution of everything that you owned is covered under the will or in a memorandum that can form a part of your will. Other than a spouse, there are no specific requirements regarding the person to whom you must leave any part of your estate. You may provide specific gifts to individual family members, friends, employees, or charities. Without a will, the state's intestate law will control this distribution. Given that the intestate laws do not deal with most individuals' situation, it is surprising that most people have not addressed the distribution of their assets by executing a will.

In the case of Linwood and Jordan, mentioned in Chapter 1, if either were to die without a will, the survivor would receive nothing under the intestate laws since they were not married. The intestate laws, like the one in Pennsylvania, only leave assets to heirs, those individuals related by marriage or in the decedent's blood line. The survivor may not even be able to serve as administrator of the estate if other family members should raise a challenge. A will or other form of advance planning is the only way that either Linwood or Jordan could distribute assets to each other at death.

The will can serve to control the destiny of your assets. In fact, you are in the best position to determine your desires and to express them clearly and unambiguously in a will. It takes a tremendous burden off family members to know your specific intent. There is no guess work regarding your last wishes. When there is uncertainty, time and money are unnecessarily expended. If you fail to provide direction on distribution of your assets, settlement of your estate could be tied up in court. If you do not want chaos and, more importantly, do not want your estate dwindled away in contested deliberation, plan ahead with the help of a professional in the field of estate planning.

A fourth and final role of your will is to control and protect the assets you leave to your beneficiaries. Therefore, your will can be as simple or as complex as you desire. Whether the will is complex or simple is not always directly linked to the net worth of your estate. Anyone can provide for periodic payments to beneficiaries instead of providing for a simple immediate distribution of the assets upon death. By controlling the distribution of your beneficiary's inheritance, you can protect the assets from bankruptcy, lawsuits, divorce settlement, and other creditors of the beneficiary. Further, do you want conditional payments or unconditional distributions? Do you have special instructions for certain assets like heirlooms, collectibles, or family pets? Are there family members with special needs to address? Are there individuals who must be located before any distribution is made? The list can go on and on depending upon your requirements to control and protect your assets.

In light of the foregoing, in Linwood's and Jordan's situation, as an unmarried couple, failure to plan will impact the situation of their special needs son Julian. Without a will, upon the death of either Linwood or Jordan, their assets would be distributed outright to Julian.

As a result, with assets in his name, he may no longer qualify for programs that have been meeting his needs over the last years. Such a disruption could represent a significant setback to Julian's progress. An option that Linwood and Jordan may want to consider is the Special Needs Trust discussed in Chapter 8.

What Other Ways Can Assets be Distributed at Death?

Some people feel a will is unnecessary. There are ways, other than a will, to transfer property when you die and thus avoid probate. This may be one of the reasons most people do not have a will. However, the potential that some property is missed under a will substitute is significant. Further, the substitutes for a will, in some cases, do not provide the benefits that may have been attributed to them. You, therefore, need to be well advised prior to making a decision not to have any form of a will.

One will substitute is the living revocable trust. It requires that all assets you owned be transferred to and retitled in the name of the trust. The question that I ask when reviewing an old, previously executed trust document is "What assets does the trust own?" The answers vary. I have encountered situations in which individuals have failed to transfer any assets into their trust. An unfunded trust is like having no trust at all. In some cases, some assets were overlooked. If any asset is missed, which often happens with assets acquired after the initial retitling, then such assets would not pass in accordance with the trust. The asset would be subject to the intestate laws of your state. Therefore, you would have failed to avoid probate, which is one of the essential benefits of having a trust. Further, many people fail to realize that a living revocable trust does not avoid inheritance tax. Inheritance tax on the property transferred under the trust at your death would be due.

Another will substitute is joint ownership. This occurs by adding another person's name to your deed, bank account, or brokerage account. Many people try to avoid probate and the need for a will by holding all of their assets jointly with their children. People spend unnecessary efforts trying to make sure all the joint accounts remain equally distributed among their children. However, this may not work in accomplishing their goals. Their efforts can be defeated by a long-term illness of the parent or the death of a child. A will can be a much simpler means of ensuring one's wishes about how assets should be distributed.

It is also important to note that with joint ownership, your assets would be partly owned by your children or any other person you may add to your property. Any creditor of your children or the other person could obtain access to your property. Further, you could not sell your real estate without the participation of the joint owner.

A third form of a will substitute is beneficiary designations. You have to remember to add or remove individuals based upon your intent for distribution at your death. On more than one occasion, I have found ex-spouses still designated as beneficiary under life insurance policies and retirement plans when that clearly was no longer the intent. Many people forget to consider updating their beneficiary designations. Review all your beneficiary designation forms when updating the distribution of your assets.

Assets that pass under a will substitute like the trust, joint ownership, or beneficiary designation are considered non-probate assets and are not subject to the probate process. However, with the exception of insurance, taxes are still due on non-probate assets. You want to make sure the beneficiaries under the will are not saddled with paying the full amount of tax on the non-probate assets. It is important then to have correct tax language incorporated in your will.

Even given all of the will substitutes, it is still best to engage in an overall estate planning process to make sure you coordinate the distribution of your assets. If the will only needs to be a "pour-over" (as when you use a trust) or needs to serve as a compliment to the other will substitutes, then such can be determined during an estate planning review.

Conclusion

Because I see the complexities that result from not having a will, I am always surprised that most people do not have one. But just as problematic is not having an updated will. An old will may no longer meet the person's changed circumstances and may not address new tax planning opportunities. As simple and as cost-effective as it might be to change or update a will, people still are not updating their wills or periodically reviewing their wills. That is why it is even more important to seek out an estate planning attorney or other professional who will not only prepare an initial will but remind you to update it periodically. It has to be on someone's radar, if not yours, to address this issue, or it will not get done.

I have found in my practice there are several triggering events that lead a person to make or update a will. Among the younger individuals, the need for a will becomes most pressing when children are born. An important question for new parents is what happens to my child if I should die while they are minors. They can provide the answer to that question by making a will. Another triggering event for making a will is after the purchase of a home. Many feel at that time they have something worth leaving to someone. Aging is also a triggering event. For the elderly, the will represents the settling of their estate. There is generally more at stake to protect and preserve for future generations.

It is not always the case that an Egyptian tomb was sealed for all eternity on the day of its owner's funeral. On the contrary, historians report forays by individuals and large-scale pillaging of ancient tombs. In modern times, we have heirs who appear seeking inclusion in your estate when you clearly would not have provided for them had you put something in writing. Don't let another form of tomb robbing occur with your estate. Whether concerns of modern day tomb robbing serves as a triggering event for you or whether getting married, having children, purchasing a home, acquiring assets, inheriting wealth, or aging does, you should know it is never too early to plan; however, it can be too late if you wait.

4: Living Wills

Terri Schiavo

In 2005, the Terri Schiavo case received national attention. It was a case dealing with the withdrawal of life support from a terminally ill person. There were no specific written instructions regarding life support provided by Terri Schiavo prior to her terminal state. Her husband and her parents could not agree on what would have been her preference regarding life support. As a result, the parents challenged the husband's decision to remove her feeding tube. During a seven-year period, the dispute involved politicians, advocacy groups, the Florida legislature, Congress, the Florida courts, and finally the United States Supreme Court. The entire nation and the world followed the extensive national and international media coverage in the final days leading to the decision to remove the feeding tube on March of 2005.

By the time the feeding tube was removed, the legal history alone around the Schiavo case included several appeals, numerous motions, petitions, and hearings in the Florida courts; several suits in Federal District Court; Florida legislation struck down by the Supreme Court of Florida; a subpoena by a congressional committee to qualify Schiavo for witness protection; federal legislation and several denials of certiorari (a means of gaining review by a higher court) from the Supreme Court of the United States. This national public debate did not have to happen. Written instructions expressing Terri Schiavo's wishes would have helped resolve or even avoid the conflict. Instead, a very private and personal tragedy became a public affair. The courts, a divided family, and a divided nation had to decide the ultimate fate of Terri Schiavo.

A year after the Schiavo case brought national attention to the subject of living wills, I conducted a survey and found that 69% of the local population still did not have a living will. Age did not matter, though the older population was slightly more prone to address this topic than those much younger. The results of the survey confirmed that most people are not making living wills a priority. Even with the incredible media coverage surrounding the case, many people, though educated on the topic, just have not been moved to action by executing a living will. I surmise that any increase in other parts of the region or nation, even now, is minimal. However, I continue to remind readers that you can not execute a living will when incapacitated by a medical emergency. I encourage you to take the critical step to make the living will a part of getting your estate planning done.

What is a Living Will?

A living will is the most common form of written instructions pertaining to the life support issues addressed in the Schiavo case. It is used to express your desires pertaining to life support for end-stage medical conditions or a permanently unconscious state. It also allows you to name a person, sometimes referred to as your surrogate, to speak the terms of the living will when you no longer can.

The living will serves as an important estate planning document. During your lifetime, you establish the quality of your life. During an end-stage medical condition, your living will allows you to determine the quality of your end of life. You can express prior to such an event your desires and therefore, help to alleviate any potential conflict.

A living will does not address all health-related matters. It only addresses end-stage medical conditions or a state of permanent unconsciousness, such as an irreversible coma or an irreversible vegetative state. There also has to be no realistic hope of recovery. Without life support, death will result. Whether such a situation represents your circumstances is determined by your physician and generally another attending physician. The type of life support that is generally addressed by your living will includes mechanical respiration, cardiac resuscitation, tube feeding, or other artificial forms of nutrition or hydration. This is not an exhaustive list but merely serves as an example. With modern technology, the forms of life support continue to advance. A discussion with your physician would be helpful in understanding the many options that are available and that you may want to address.

In fact, your living will can be very complex or simple. It can provide specific details regarding your life support alternatives, or it can merely state that you do not want heroic efforts used if you are in an end of life state. Whether your living will is complex or simple, it should be explained to and understood by your surrogate.

Role of the Surrogate

The surrogate is the individual you name under your living will to represent your decision regarding life support. It is important to name someone who can address your preference consistent with the terms of the living will. The person named as your surrogate under the living will should be someone whom you trust and who is aware of your preferences regarding life support. Your surrogate has to be a person who is able to adhere to your directive regarding your life support preference whether they agree with your decision or not. The surrogate will be privy to your private medical information so that they can make an informed decision on your behalf.

It is important to understand that accepting the role of surrogate is a very personal decision, and sometimes the person closest to you may not be able to serve in this role. For example, in one case a wife could not follow the express wishes of her husband's living will, and the daughter had to intervene through the courts to get the living will upheld. That is why a very frank conversation with those you love is very important in choosing your surrogate. You want to know in advance that they will adhere to your dictates.

In your surrogate's decision-making process, there may be many questions. They must first follow the clearly expressed terms of your living will. If specific medical treatment is not covered, your surrogate can reflect upon your preferences and values whether they stem from your religious or moral beliefs. Overall, your surrogate must act in your best interest.

Living Will Formats

There are many forms of living wills available for your use. Some states, like Pennsylvania, provide a recommended format under their statutes. Some hospitals or even physician associations have adopted recommended formats for individuals to consider. A format known as the Five Wishes, created with the help of the medical and legal profession, has been introduced nationally and is acceptable for use in many states.

Additionally, your estate planning attorney can share alternative formats available to you and discuss their application to your overall plan. Your attorney can also help you develop your own format. Whether you choose a form document or express your intent in your own words with the assistance of your estate planning attorney or healthcare professional, your living will alleviates the pain and anguish between family members in making such a final decision.

Role of Medical Professionals

The role of your physician or healthcare professional in this area is invaluable. The landscape of ethics and end-of-life care has changed so significantly and continues to evolve. Some physicians therefore consider it their role to help facilitate your decision by listening, communicating, and advising on end-of-life care. It is just good medical practice for your physician to discuss these issues with you.

More and more legislative direction is being provided in this field to help facilitate these discussions with your doctor. It is important, whether or not you worked with your doctor when creating your living will, that you advise your physician of your preference regarding life support as well as make your living will a part of your medical file. It is your attending physician who will determine your end-stage medical condition or permanent unconscious state and may be the first to communicate your condition to your surrogate. Understanding the terms of your living will is not only helpful to your surrogate, but it is your doctor who is best equipped with the expertise to address any medical treatment questions raised by your surrogate.

Legal Requirements for a Living Will

Like a will, you have to be at least eighteen years of age to make a living will. In many states, the living will has to be signed by you and witnessed by two people. You have to be competent and of sound mind to execute a living will. It is best when you are not under a lot of stress and can take the time to give this formality the attention it deserves, if not just for you, then for the benefit of those you love.

Like any other estate planning documents you create, you can change your living will at anytime. You must retrieve and destroy all copies you may have given out, especially those placed in your medical files. If your living will is very specific regarding treatment, you may want to update it by addressing any changes in medical technology.

Difference From Healthcare Power of Attorney

The living will is not to be confused with the healthcare power of attorney. The healthcare power of attorney pertains to all medical situations you may encounter during your lifetime. Most of your medical situations will not be life threatening. The living will only pertains to end-of-life situations.

Generally, I recommend that you have both a living will and a healthcare power of attorney. I also recommend that the surrogate under your living will serve as the agent under the healthcare power of attorney since both cover health-related matters, and you do not want a different person to handle end-of-life issues if he or she has not been involved throughout your specific medical condition. If you have different people, one serving as the agent under the healthcare power of attorney and another serving as the surrogate under your living will, then the surrogate under the living will would not have been directly privy to the medical situation leading to your end-stage condition. The main point is that you want to assure consistency in the handling of your medical situation, and naming the same person provides that consistency in many cases. An informed decision regarding your healthcare requires that your surrogate/agent has all the information needed.

5: Healthcare Power of Attorney

Gliding on their sled across the glistening ice crystals, the three little girls giggled happily. Their father, strong and heroic, had turned their expansive backyard into a winter wonderland with a little help from nature. The ice storm had created a perfectly safe adventure for Jack and his girls. He skated across the ice pulling their sled effortlessly, laughing with them all the way. It was moments like this that Jack relished. It was also moments like this that Jack lamented.

Remember Jack, single father raising three young children after the loss of his wife. Jack has always been very close to his girls, and now he is even more protective of them and worries about their future if something should also happen to him. His mother Mary works tirelessly caring for Charles, Jack's father, who has been diagnosed with a mentally debilitating form of Alzheimer's. To further complicate Jack's life, the doctors have advised that his father's disease could be hereditary.

Jack realizes that he has to be concerned about the potential hereditary aspect of his father's illness. He will need someone to handle all aspects of his personal affairs if he becomes incapacitated or disabled. One important aspect will be his medical treatment. If his physicians are unable to communicate with him, who does he want them to turn to for answers? There will be hard decisions that Jack will have to consider now so that he can indicate his preferences in a healthcare power of attorney and can share such preferences with the person he designates as his agent.

What is a Healthcare Power of Attorney?

While the living will provides guidance as to your wishes when you are at an end-of-life stage, the healthcare power of attorney addresses the overwhelming majority of cases that fall somewhere between an end-stage medical condition and everything else. It is a legally binding document enabling another person to act on your behalf. It is used by your agent whenever your physician determines that you lack the ability to understand or to make or communicate a decision regarding your health care.

Upon regaining capacity, as may be determined by your healthcare provider, you resume your authority to handle your health care matters. Your agent has no authority over your health care when you have the capacity to handle such matters yourself.

However, the healthcare power of attorney will become effective again if your incapacity recurs. You have an opportunity to evaluate your agent's effectiveness during any incapacity. As always, remember you can change the healthcare power of attorney as well as the designated agent based upon your experiences, changing circumstances, and evolving healthcare matters.

Legal Requirements for the Healthcare Power of Attorney

One of the big questions for many people is when to have a healthcare power of attorney drawn up. Like the other essential estate planning documents, now is the time. You have to be at least eighteen years of age to make a healthcare power of attorney. In many states, the healthcare power of attorney has to be signed by you and witnessed by two people. You have to be competent and of sound mind to execute a healthcare power of attorney. The best time to execute a healthcare power of attorney is when you are not under a lot of stress and can take the time to give this formality the attention it deserves.

Like any other estate planning documents you create, you can change your healthcare power of attorney at anytime. You must retrieve and destroy all copies you may have given out, especially those placed in your medical files.

Whether you are young, middle-aged, or a senior, the healthcare power of attorney helps take the question work out of your immediate treatment options. The more you plan in advance, the better it serves you. You may have dependent children or a flourishing business. You can address what happens in those situations if you are incapacitated. Therefore, when a healthcare need arises and someone has been designated to facilitate your preferences, normalcy can soon return to those situations and other aspects of your life. When you are incapacitated, you want the least amount of disruption as possible. Upon regaining capacity, you can more effortlessly resume your lifestyle.

Setting Up the Healthcare Power of Attorney

When you meet with your estate planning attorney to draw up your healthcare power of attorney and other essential documents, you can discuss the specific powers that should and may be granted to your agent. You may even want to address specific medical areas given your medical situation. You can answer questions now that may be posed to your agent in the future. Decisions made when you are not in an emergency or crisis situation are more thoughtful, and they help avoid potential regrets. You can make simple what could become complex without advance planning. It is up to you to take care of you. Advance planning definitely helps.

Further, as part of your advance planning, it is a good idea to ask your physician for guidance in addressing potential medical issues. You and your physician are in the best position to know the health issues that are likely to arise. With your physician's help, you can cover those items most critical to you. Once this is done, any updating would only have to address new health issues.

The healthcare power of attorney is your document. It is not your physician's or your estate planning attorney's. They both only serve as additional resources to you in the advance planning process.

Who Should Serve as Your Agent?

You can authorize an agent to act on your behalf under your healthcare power of attorney. Your agent should be someone you trust. Generally, if you are married, you would name your spouse as your agent. Your spouse is generally aware of your health issues and can be readily available to address an emergency or a health crisis. Generally, a spouse is in the best position to understand the health issues leading up to an incapacity. Even in the absence of a designation, your spouse may be given priority as the person with whom the medical profession would consult regarding your health matters. Therefore, if your spouse's views on health matters differ from your own, it would be prudent to name another person as agent.

If your spouse is not the individual you want to designate as your agent or, as in Jack's case, you do not have a spouse, then you can designate another family member, including your adult child or grandchild, parent, brother, or sister as your agent. You can also designate a friend. However, it can not be your attending physician nor an owner, operator, or employee of a healthcare provider where you are receiving care unless such individual is related to you. Your agent should have knowledge of your preferences and values based on, but not limited to, religious and moral beliefs to assess how you would make healthcare decisions. Therefore, it is someone whom you are willing to give access to your medical information if you were incapacitated. Choosing an agent is a very important decision and should only be done with adequate thought and deliberation.

Role of Your Agent

Once you decide who should serve as your agent, the next step is to obtain the person's concurrence to serve in that capacity. Do they understand the role that they would be assuming? Can they proceed in accordance with your desires? Can they be available to serve if the need should arise?

Your agent serves in a fiduciary capacity on your behalf. This is a legal standard that means that any and everything he or she does on your behalf must be done in your best interest. An agent acting as fiduciary cannot take his or her interest regarding your healthcare above yours. In other words, your agent can not allow his or her interest or preferences to override your specific directive to them. As long as the agent fulfills all fiduciary responsibilities, the agent is not liable to anyone for actions done on your behalf. If your agent fails to act in your best interest, he or she can be held liable by you or your estate for failure to do so.

After you have selected a person who accepts the role as your agent, then you want to share a copy of the healthcare power of attorney with him or her. Your original healthcare power of attorney, as well as your other estate planning documents, should be maintained where your agent can access the appropriate document whenever it is needed. It will be needed if you become incapacitated, and your medical records have to be shared with someone other than you.

Powers of Your Agent

Your healthcare power of attorney allows you to appoint an agent to address medically-related issues, which would include allowing your agent to authorize the type and length of medical treatment. Making anatomical gifts can be a part of your healthcare power of attorney if you are an organ donor or would like to have your remains used for medical purposes. Your agent determines and authorizes your admission to the hospital or a nursing home and determines at what point hospice care is considered. You can even provide specific preferences on the facilities for your admission for health care. It is one less thing left to chance. Whatever you would be called upon to do if you were not incapacitated, your agent can do under your healthcare power attorney.

Health Insurance Portability and Accountability Act "HIPAA"

You are the only one entitled to your personal medical information, files, or records. Healthcare professionals and healthcare institutions are required to maintain the privacy of your confidential medical information under the Health Insurance Portability and Accountability Act,

"HIPAA." Most of us have received a HIPAA disclosure statement while visiting our healthcare professionals. Under HIPAA, such individuals or institutions can be held liable for any failure to adhere to this legal requirement. But what happens if you are incapacitated and your healthcare professional can not communicate with you regarding your treatment preference? This is one of the times that a healthcare power of attorney would be important. The healthcare power of attorney allows you to authorize someone to have access to your medical records. This would be the person with whom your physician may communicate. Therefore, it would be important to share a copy of your healthcare power of attorney with your physician. It can form a part of your medical files. Your agent is allowed access to the medical history on your condition provided in your medical files. With such access, your agent or personal representative can make an informed decision regarding your medical treatment.

Guardianship

The healthcare power of attorney is also an essential way to avoid a determination of guardianship by the court. You control the terms and conditions of the healthcare power of attorney. You have the power to designate an agent. It is imperative that you appoint someone to make decisions regarding your health as well as your financial affairs (see Chapter 6, General Power of Attorney) while you are well. When you become incapacitated, it is too late. You are no longer legally eligible to make an informed decision regarding your affairs. It is at this time that the courts may intervene. It could be a medical crisis situation. There is no one available to address the situation for you or those who are available disagree. The simple process of executing a healthcare power of attorney could prevent what will now become a time-consuming and costly guardianship process. If there is no agreement among those whom you would have potentially appointed as your agent, then the person appointed by the court as your guardian could be a stranger to you and to your loved ones. Your thoughtful action now can help avoid this scenario.

Mental Health

Your physical as well as mental health can be addressed by your healthcare power of attorney. As we live longer, more issues regarding mental capacity arise. From Alzheimer's, dementia, to other forms of senility; we have to address matters that are now becoming common-place. In fact, there are facilities that are just addressing specific forms of mental illness because the one-size-fits-all approach no longer works. The same is true for how each individual may want his or her mental issues addressed. This is your time, when you are mentally competent, to explore the options available to you and dictate your own care. For example, your agent can consent or refuse to consent to psychiatric care, including the right to voluntary commitment to a psychiatric care facility if it becomes necessary.

Given the extensive nature of mental health issues in recent times, I recommend that a separate mental health power of attorney be executed as part of your estate plan. If there is a family history of mental illness, or you have been diagnosed with a mental problem that could progress to incapacity, you can be more definitive in your mental health power of attorney regarding your desires. You can indicate your choice of treatment facility. Your preferences for psychiatric treatment, electroconvulsive therapy, and experimental studies or drug trials are also essential to include in your mental health power of attorney.

If you have specific religious beliefs, your mental health power of attorney and healthcare power of attorney serve as vehicles to assure your religious preferences are addressed. Others need to know and understand your religious intent regarding lifesaving measures. Additional information or instructions to consider placing in your mental health power of attorney include dietary requirements and the type of intervention in the event of a crisis as well as other mental health care matters of importance to you.

Long-term Care

The healthcare power of attorney is like long-term care insurance. We hope we never have to use it, but if we do, it will prove to be one of the best uses of our time and money. Both long-term care insurance and the healthcare power of attorney are about addressing future long-term care before it is required.

Another option that is now available and that many individuals are pursing for their long-term care needs are long-term care facilities or continuing care facilities. These facilities provide a continuum of care, from independent living to assisted living, to nursing home care, to hospice care. The arrangements are varied so you should inquire into several to determine what options might serve you well. As we live longer with the potential for some healthcare assistance being required at some point in our longer life span, knowing your options is the best way to plan and be prepared.

Conclusion

Most of us will no longer just lead a healthy life and then die of old age. Given that we are living much longer, the likelihood of illness, short or long term, is more prevalent. The healthcare power of attorney is an inexpensive way to help assure some consistency in your health care. You can use the document to take the guesswork out of what your preferences might be in a given health situation. Candid discussions with your agent and physician now can reduce much anguish later. You can discuss new treatments that might address your particular health issues or those in your personal family history. You can even address health problems specific to your ethnic heritage. You may have a preference for a specific treatment or want alternative health options pursued before more traditional remedies are attempted. Let the preparation of your healthcare power of attorney serve to document your health care preferences and thereby ease the decision-making process for your loved ones in the future.

I have often counseled clients who have not even considered the impact of any illness, let alone a mental illness, on their assets. Once they know that a significant amount of assets can be misdirected, mismanaged, or even depleted as the result of a physical or mental illness, they begin advance planning.

Jack has begun to consider his future health issues for the sake of his children. He realizes that neither person closest to him, his mother nor father, can help him in a time of crisis. His elderly mother is already overly strained with the care of Charles, Jack's father. However, Jack does not want to have his children subjected to a court's determination. Therefore, he is carefully evaluating the options available to him. Maybe a close friend could serve, or even as his children age, he could prepare the oldest to be his agent. There is no better time than now for Jack to make the right choices for his future health issues.

6: General Power of Attorney

W e sometimes think that the people closest to us will take care of us in our time of need. Sometimes this is true, and sometimes it is not. The latter may be our own fault. We often make the assumption that our intentions are universally known and accepted. However, we have taken no action to validate this broad assumption. Is it because we do not understand the importance? Is it because we do not have the time or are too busy to take the time? Is it because we feel we will never need help? Sometimes our focus is on everyone else but ourselves.

For Linwood and Jordan, their primary focus has been on the needs of Julian, their adopted special needs son. Now, at twenty-six, Julian is learning to live independently. Though they have appropriately provided for Julian in the event of their death, Linwood and Jordan have not addressed the possibility of their own incapacity or disability. If either or both of them should become incapacitated or disabled, who would serve as their agent? The assumption that one spouse can act on behalf of another (though this is not necessarily universal and clearly is not for all actions) is not applicable to unmarried individuals, like Linwood and Jordan. Without specific instructions, they could not serve as each other's agent.

What is a Durable Power of Attorney?

A "durable" power of attorney means that the power of attorney remains in effect during an incapacity or disability. In Pennsylvania, it is specifically provided by law that the power of attorney remains in effect during an incapacity or disability unless specifically provided otherwise in the power of attorney. Therefore, it is not necessary to use the term durable. Many practitioners refer to their power of attorney as a general power of attorney, which, given its durable nature, is the perfect tool for incapacity or disability planning. As a key document in incapacity or disability planning, the general power of attorney allows you to plan a smooth transition to your agent upon your incapacity or disability. It allows your agent to seamlessly administer your financial and business affairs.

Legal Requirements for the General Power of Attorney

Under Pennsylvania law, you are required to sign that you understand the nature and significance of the power of attorney. You also sign the power of attorney and have it acknowledged by a notary. Your agent does not need to be present when you execute your power of attorney; he or she signs and dates it when it needs to be used. Your agent's signature does not have to be notarized.

It is important that you have more than one original power of attorney. In order to affect many transactions, an original (not a copy) is required to allow your agent to sign on your behalf. It is a good practice to have at least three originals. If you misplace one, there are others available for use. In some cases, an original power of attorney has to be filed along with the document signed by your agent under the power of attorney. An example of this would be a real estate deed filing. Having more than one original power of attorney alleviates complexities that may arise with having just one.

Who Should Serve as Your Agent?

Designating someone that you trust is the first and most important criteria for selecting your agent. Special expertise or a particular profession is not necessary. A trusted person can be relied upon to obtain the necessary assistance, advice, and guidance when and if needed. You want someone who will look out for your best interest.

Also, what has proven in my practice to be just as important as trust is appointing someone who can make difficult decisions in your best interest and follow through on those decisions. You do not want someone who can not handle stressful situations or not be able to take control of your affairs when it is clear you are no longer capable.

Once you have identified a trusted individual who can handle stressful situations, a third consideration, but not as important as the first two, is appointing someone who has knowledge of your business affairs. It will make it easier for the person to handle matters for you. Knowledge of your business and financial affairs is a plus but is not essential.

If the person you decide to select does not know your affairs, then you have several options towards alleviating this deficiency. First, you can begin to share information regarding your business and financial affairs with your trusted friend or family member. Second, you can have instructions available regarding your affairs that your agent can access upon your incapacity or disability. Such documentation could be maintained in the same location as your general power of attorney. Finally, if you work with professional advisors in handling your business and financial affairs, you can direct your agent to work with them if you should become incapacitated or disabled. Such a directive can be provided in your general power of attorney.

If you have a business, it is important that you have contingency plans in place for incapacity or disability. In such a case, you should have a succession plan in place. This will assure the viability of your business. You do not want the business to decline if you should be unavailable. Business succession planning is an entire book in itself. However, as part of estate planning, you want to coordinate your personal and business affairs for consistency in handling.

In many cases, your spouse will hold the power of attorney. Your spouse generally handles financial affairs without having a power of attorney because when assets are held jointly, a power of attorney is not required. This applies to writing checks and withdrawing funds from a jointly held bank or brokerage account. However, separately titled bank accounts, brokerage accounts, and other assets would require a power of attorney even for a spouse to handle your affairs. This would also apply to job related assets such as 401(k), 403(b), and other retirement accounts.

Generally, you want to name a primary agent under the power of attorney and an alternate agent. Your primary agent may be unable or unavailable to serve under the power of attorney. The alternate could be another family member if you are trying to delegate roles among a number of family members. Many people try to make sure close trusted family members are involved in important decisions. You could also choose a friend or an institution as your alternate agent. The main thing to remember is that you want to facilitate your financial and business affairs through your power of attorney. Therefore, naming an alternate agent avoids the potential of not having someone available.

Some people choose to name joint agents. However, joint agents can create other complications. If you name more than one person as your primary agent, all of your agents would have to agree on actions and be available to execute required documents. If there is disagreement, transactions will be delayed until agreement is reached. Even given that precautionary caveat, you may still choose to have joint agents.

You could choose two individuals or an institution and individual as your joint agents. They could serve as an integrated checks and balance system, making sure each is acting in your best interest. However, you do not want to complicate the process to your disadvantage. Unless you are absolutely certain that the individuals you name can work in harmony, my recommendation would be to choose only one trusted agent to serve under the power of attorney. As an alternative, you could name an individual as your agent but require in your power of attorney that the person seek advice and guidance from another person, a professional, or an institution. Even though the final decision will be with the named agent, others are made aware of the potential action and can give their input. It is always good to have provisions in place to protect your interests without creating complexity.

In any event, whether the agent under your general power of attorney is your spouse, another family member, friend, or business associate, you have to advise them of your intent to appoint them as your agent and make sure they are willing to serve in that capacity. This role should never come as a surprise to anyone.

Role of Your Agent

Your agent is under a fiduciary role to act in your best interest. This is a legal standard of care which prohibits the agent from acting in his or her own interest. All action taken must be done with your best interest as the priority. Failure of your agent to act in your best interest could result in your agent being held liable for any damages that result from such failure. Your agent can be sued for failing to perform as your fiduciary. Any checks and balances that you may put in place, such as a joint agent or someone serving in an advisory role, can help determine whether your agent is performing appropriately. If your agent is not performing appropriately, then litigation is available to those who may be overseeing your agent's actions.

Powers of Your Agent

The general power of attorney gives your agent broad powers to handle your property and affairs. The type of authority provided includes buying or selling real estate, personal property, stocks, bonds, insurance policies; handling tax matters, claims, banking transactions, litigation, gifting; setting up trusts, brokerage accounts; and engaging in retirement plan transactions. These are just a few examples of the types of transactions your agent may handle on your behalf.

It is imperative that you make sure the power of attorney you have created will meet your needs. How broad your power of attorney should be depends upon the nature of the areas covered in your personal and business affairs. You want to make sure the power of attorney covers the transactions you need to address. I have found in my practice when reviewing clients' documents that their power of attorney was limited in ways that they did not realize. You should engage a professional to plan your estate and not rely on standard forms that might be confusing or lack clarity. Having your agent find out your document is not sufficient when the agent needs to use it is much too late.

You can, however, intentionally limit the powers granted under your power of attorney. You can limit its use to a specific purpose. For example, your power of attorney can just be for a real estate transaction. Once the transaction has occurred, the authority under the power of attorney ceases. This could happen when you are unable or unavailable to complete a real estate transaction, but you are still interested in moving forward with the purchase. You could, for example, be traveling out of the country or otherwise be predisposed. In such a case, you can authorize an agent to sign on your behalf.

Handling banking transactions is another example of a power of attorney for a specific purpose. Such a power of attorney can be given via a standard issued banking form. The agent is only authorized to handle your banking affairs.

Springing Power of Attorney

Unless specified otherwise, the general power of attorney is effective immediately. However, it is wise to maintain the document within your possession. It is not necessary nor do I advise my clients to give the document to their agent. Your agent, however, should be advised of its location and given the necessary information to retrieve it when needed for your benefit.

If you do not want your general power of attorney to be effective immediately, then it could become effective at a specified future time or upon the occurrence of a specified contingency. Once the designated triggering event arises, the general power of attorney can be used. In this case, the document is referred to as a springing power of attorney. It assures you that the general power of attorney will not be effective unless a specific triggering event has occurred. It provides many with a sense of security that the document will not be used improperly.

Generally, the triggering event or condition precedent to the activation of the springing power of attorney is the certification by your physician of your incapacity or a disability since that is generally when you want someone to act for you. The certification has to be attached to the power of attorney so that anyone relying on its use is aware that you are in fact incapacitated or disabled. When you regain capacity, the springing power of attorney is no longer effective. It can, however, be reactivated upon any future incapacity or disability.

A general power of attorney that does not have a triggering event or condition precedent could be used without your permission or knowledge if the agent has possession or can get possession of it. That is why it is crucial that trust serves as a key criteria when choosing an agent.

Guardianship

If you fail to plan a transition during any incapacity or disability, there could be protracted and involved legal proceedings to determine who will handle your affairs during such period. These court proceedings are required because you failed to plan. Ultimately, the agent appointed as part of any court proceedings could be someone you do not know, especially if there is no agreement among close family members or if no one is willing to serve in that capacity. In such situations, the court appointed agent, referred to as a guardian, is selected from the court's own list of potential individuals or organizations available to serve.

Do you want to subject your personal and business affairs to individuals who are unknown to you? You have a choice if you act before incapacity or disability. Since we do not know when such incapacity or disability may occur, it is important to plan in advance.

Conclusion

Once your power of attorney has been created and executed, you want to keep them in a safe place along with your other estate planning documents. This would be in either a safety deposit box at your banking institution or a safe at your home. The safe should be fire and water proof. It may be a combination lock or key. The safe could be a fixture in the wall, bolted to the floor, or free standing. Another option for the security of the original estate planning document is in your attorney's office, provided there is capacity and a secure location.

For your power of attorney, your attorney may only need to maintain one original just in case you lose or misplace your originals. Unlike the will and living will, your general power of attorney or healthcare power of attorney will be used more often. Therefore, maintaining possession within your immediate control is best.

Your power of attorney is an essential estate planning document during your lifetime. Upon your death, it ceases to operate. The individual designated as your agent no longer has any authority. The executor named under your will or trustee named under your trust will become responsible for handling your affairs. Estate planning involves creating critical documents essential while you are living as well as essential upon your death.

7: Living and Testamentary Trusts

M y estate planning practice focuses on people. Though many of my clients are interested in learning about the latest sophisticated techniques to reduce taxes at death, their primary concerns with me quickly turn to the personal, non-tax side of estate planning. Today's clients want to know that the wealth they leave their children is wisely used to benefit their heirs and not something that ruins their incentive to work or achieve. Wealth should be an opportunity. It should not serve to cripple and stifle initiative, creativity, and productivity. The tabloids often follow those of inherited wealth leading meaningless and sometime destructive lifestyles. Ensuring that their heirs have more meaningful values is of critical importance to clients who realize that giving their children substantial wealth may not truly benefit them in the long run.

After the phone call from their daughter Julia relaying yet another irresponsible escapade, Eve and Bob met with an estate planning attorney to discuss their options. They realized that some of their prior estate planning was in need of review and revision. Their primary concern at the present time was to make sure the assets left to Julia were properly managed for her benefit and protected from her creditors. They were even hopeful that their wealth could at some point in Julia's life make her less self-centered and more motivated to make a difference.

Though all the answers that Eve and Bob may seek for Julia can not be addressed with a magic estate planning document, there are ways that estate planning can help heirs, like Julia, become financially literate and emotionally responsible. One method is for Eve and Bob to create a trust, appointing Julia, their adult child as co-trustee. This situation can be treated as a financial apprenticeship.

Eve's and Bob's estate planning attorney can help them assemble a team under the trust, consisting of the attorney, an accountant, and a financial advisor to help Julia learn the basics of investing and fiscal responsibility.

A thoughtfully drafted trust can also help to steer Julia's life in the right direction. Trusts can be set up to cover expenses for major life events, like education, home purchase, or even a wedding when the time is right for Julia who has already been engaged twice. At the same time, the terms and conditions of the trust can be set up to help Julia be responsible for basic and ongoing living expenses, thus helping to develop and instill emotional maturity.

It seems that parents, regardless of their financial circumstances, get a true sense of satisfaction if they can provide a terrific launching off point for their children so that they may lead fulfilling lives. For the affluent, like Eve and Bob, the tax savings that can be achieved by using certain techniques to accomplish that is often viewed as a bonus.

What a trust is exactly and the mechanics of its operation is fairly straightforward. The text that follows will demonstrate how the trust works for you and your heirs. With this knowledge, you can then seek professional guidance for the implementation of your estate plan.

What is a Trust?

A trust is a legal agreement used in estate planning that provides for the management and distribution of your property when you die. You, through your attorney, create a written document called a Declaration of Trust or Trust Agreement, whereby you, referred to as the settlor or grantor, transfer property to another person, called the trustee, who holds the property for the benefit of another person, called the beneficiary. The obligation of your trustee is to conserve and protect assets transferred to the trust and to collect income and distribute or accumulate it as prescribed in the trust instrument.

A trust can be a living trust or a testamentary trust. The typical living trust is revocable and amendable by you, the settlor, during your lifetime. You are also the trustee and beneficiary of the trust during your lifetime. As trustee, you can manage and control the trust property; as beneficiary, you receive all of the benefits of the trust assets. Upon your death, a successor trustee (child, friend, bank, etc.) takes over as trustee and follows your instructions, which are set forth in the trust, concerning the distribution of property and the payment of taxes and expenses.

A testamentary trust is a trust that is created in a will. There are no benefits to you, the testator (the creator of the will), or the beneficiaries during your lifetime. Once you die, the trust is created with the terms and conditions provided by you in the will. Therefore, a testamentary trust only comes into effect upon your death, while the living trust is effective prior to your death.

A properly formed and administered trust, whether living or testamentary, can provide tax planning flexibility for the beneficiaries and the necessary preservation of assets for generations.

Living Trust – Revocable or Irrevocable

A living trust can be revocable or irrevocable. A revocable living trust can be changed or revoked by you at any time. Since you still control the assets in a revocable living trust, this trust does not protect assets against creditors, who can reach any asset you can reach or control. The revocable living trust holds assets. It allows you to manage your assets during your lifetime and successor trustees to manage your assets upon your disability. It transfers assets upon your death consistent with the terms and conditions you provide.

You can serve as the initial trustee of your revocable living trust. Your successor trustee should be a trusted family member, friend, business associate, professional, or institution. Some knowledge of your financial, business, and personal affairs is helpful to provide consistency in the handling of these matters during any incapacity.

This is especially important if you place the assets of a business venture in the revocable living trust.

In contrast, an irrevocable trust can not be changed or revoked. You should not serve as the trustee under an irrevocable trust. You should name another person to serve as your trustee to help ensure that you obtain the benefits of such a trust. One such benefit is asset protection. You do not want to have any control over the assets. If you can not access the assets, neither can your creditors. Once the assets are placed in the trust, they are subject to the trust's terms and conditions, which can not be changed and are applicable during your lifetime and at your death.

An irrevocable trust is an important estate planning tool. However, you should be certain that the assets placed in the trust are not ones that you would ever need in the future. An irrevocable trust is not for everyone. You should consult a professional to determine whether your circumstances merit such a trust.

Uses of a Trust

Avoidance of Probate

Although living trusts have been around for quite some time, the general public has only recently caught on to the use of living trusts as a way to avoid the time and significant costs, in some states, of probate. Probate is a court-supervised procedure for collecting assets when a person dies, paying debts and taxes, and distributing the property to your beneficiaries (either according to the instructions you set forth in your will or as determined by state law if you die without a will).

Will Substitute

A living trust serves as a will substitute. Property placed into a living trust will pass to the beneficiaries outside of probate. The probate process is not applicable to the living trust's assets. Probate, the court procedure otherwise required to transfer assets to your beneficiaries at death, literally means to prove a will and therefore only a will is probated.

The living trust accomplishes the same thing as a will. The trust determines who will handle the distribution of the assets and who will be the beneficiaries of the assets. The trust only controls the distribution of those assets properly titled in the name of the trust.

Inheritance Tax

Even though assets distributed under a living trust will avoid probate, such assets will still be subject to a state's inheritance tax. Generally speaking, any transfer of assets as a result of death will result in inheritance taxes being due.

Asset Protection

Some trusts, i.e. irrevocable trusts, serve to protect your assets from creditors. It is imperative when creating a trust for asset protection that you relinquish control of the asset placed in the trust. Otherwise, if you have access to the asset, so will your creditors.

You can also set up a trust for the benefit of other people. For asset protection purposes, you do not want your beneficiaries to have direct access to the assets. The beneficiaries should not have the right to demand either the income or principal. All distributions must be within the sole discretion of the trustee. The creditors of your beneficiaries will therefore not have access to the assets. If the beneficiaries do not have any right to income and/or principal, then such funds can not be attached or obtained by a creditor.

In addition, you do not want the beneficiaries to be able to sell, assign, pledge, mortgage or, in any other manner encumber their interest in the trust. Your trust terms can specifically prohibit a creditor of a beneficiary from attaching the assets, seeking a forced sale of the assets, or levying against the beneficiaries' interest in the trust.

Control

Another reason for a trust is to control the manner of distribution of assets to the beneficiaries. The terms of a trust can spread the distribution of assets to beneficiaries over an extended period of time. The terms can also restrict distribution if beneficiaries fail to comply with terms and conditions imposed under the trust. You have worked long and hard to accumulate your assets so you want to make sure the assets last. A lump sum distribution to your heirs does not provide the assurance that you may need that your assets will not be wasted. A trust does provide some assurance in that area.

Disability Planning

A trust has lifetime benefits as well as benefits at death. One such lifetime benefit is disability planning. There are some types of trusts that serve well as a disability planning tool. Whether you have a business or just personal assets, you want to make sure those assets are preserved if you should become incapacitated. A living trust allows you to serve as the initial trustee managing your own assets. You name in your trust a successor trustee to serve when you are unable to manage the assets that you placed in your trust. You can provide your successor trustee broad discretion in managing your affairs for you, or you can provide the specific details regarding the handling of your assets. This can include who your successor trustee will use for managing your investment and handling your legal affairs. The specific terms and conditions delineated in the trust direct how the successor trustee must function in controlling, managing, protecting, and preserving the assets of the trust during your disability.

In the case of a business which relies upon your availability, you may want to appoint a successor trustee who is knowledgeable of your business operation, if possible. Planning is very critical to keeping a business going during your incapacity. If you have staff or colleagues in the business handling things for you, now is the time to document your process for keeping your business afloat. Stop and take the time to plan now. It will keep your future and business secure.

Real Estate – Ownership in More Than One State

Another important reason to have a trust involves owning property in more than one state. You can transfer the deed into the name of the trust. If there is a mortgage on the property, you have to determine whether consent is required from the mortgage holder and obtain such consent, where required, prior to transfer into the trust. The deed, along with the other assets in the trust, would be distributed in accordance with the terms of the trust upon your death. The assets, including those in other states, would not have to go through the probate process.

Without a trust, your estate would have to be probated in each state where property is located. This is time consuming and can be very costly. Having a trust in this type of situation can avoid a lot of anguish on the part of your loved ones. Even if you have a "pour-over" will, discussed later, it does not allow you to avoid probate for out-of-state property not placed in the trust.

Privacy

If you are not interested in the nature of your assets and the distribution of your assets becoming public, then another reason to consider a trust would be for the privacy that it affords you. Unlike a will, a trust is not a public document. A will has to be filed upon death, but a trust is not filed. In some cases, the trust, or some portions of the trust, may have to be filed with the recording of any deed transferred into the trust. However, generally, a trust provides more privacy than a will.

If a dispute should arise under a trust, however, resolution of such dispute will come under the purview of the probate court, a public domain. Having a trust drafted with clarity and specificity helps alleviate potential disputes and public scrutiny.

If any of the foregoing represent the reason for establishing your trust, then it is imperative that all assets be transferred to the trust. Once the trust is created, the process of retitling assets into the trust must begin.

Retitling

Retitling assets currently in your name into the name of the trust should begin immediately after the trust is executed. This includes changing ownership on your deeds, stocks, bonds, CDs, bank accounts, mutual funds, and business assets. The beneficiary designation under your insurance, annuities, and retirement plan should name the trust if you intend the terms of the trust to apply. For some accounts, like the retirement plan when you are married, should be reviewed with your attorney prior to naming the trust. There are spousal benefits applicable to retirement accounts that are advantageous to the spouse. Remember, assets only get in the trust if you put them there. Do not procrastinate.

When you retitle your assets into the trust, you can continue to control and manage the assets as the initial trustee. You establish an ongoing process for the effective management of those assets and do not have to seek permission to access your money from another person. You have complete control and responsibility. The trust just allows you to be more organized and systematic in handling your business and personal assets.

Pour-over Will

Even when you have a trust, there is still a need for a will. Often referred to as a "pour-over" will, it serves to pour-over into the trust any asset which was never retitled to the trust. This could have resulted from an oversight with current assets or with assets acquired after the execution of the trust, like an inheritance. If you should become incapacitated, transfer of future acquired assets could be affected and never transferred. However, if you have a power of attorney, your agent, if aware of newly acquired assets, can place assets in your trust on your behalf. If your death should result in your estate having the right to bring a wrongful death action, your estate would be entitled to the award attributable to the personal claim, i.e. pain and suffering and loss of wages, made on your behalf. The pour-over will transfers the award into your trust for distribution in accordance with the terms of the trust.

There is always the potential that some asset is overlooked, and the pour-over will provides you with the needed protection should that potentiality arise. As mentioned previously, the pour-over will does not allow you to avoid probate for out-of-state property not placed in the trust. Therefore, the importance of retitling can not be over emphasized.

8: Specific Types of Trusts - Marital Trusts and Unique Circumstances

Generally, as has been discussed in the previous chapter, there are trusts that can be created during your lifetime and those that are created at your death. Within that general context, there are many specific types of trusts created for various reasons to accomplish very defined objectives. This chapter will highlight some of the most prevalent ones used by many estate planning attorneys to address the majority of situations and circumstances that arise for families and individuals. It is important to meet with an estate planning professional to address your unique estate planning needs.

Special Needs Trusts

As a result of complications during his birth, Julian sustained permanent mental and physical limitations. Though Julian has been blind (one particular result) since birth, there is much that he can see. Through his imagination and the support of Mainstream For Life, a state funded program, Julian has created a world that works perfectly for him. At 26, he still maintains a childlike wonderment and trust for everyone he encounters in his life. Fortunately, his home and work environment support the person that Julian has become.

Linwood and Jordan (Julian's adoptive parents) realize that they both have contributed to the stable and productive life that Julian enjoys. They also realize the importance of the routine, familiarity, and normalcy provided by the state funded programs. They often worry about not being around to keep Julian safe. However, they also realize that they will not always be there to watch over him. Their focus has turned to how to sustain what has been developed for Julian when they both die. A part of that answer is the special needs trust.

A special needs trust, sometimes referred to as a supplemental needs trust, is critical to protecting Julian's health and well-being. The purpose of the special needs trust is to assure continuity of care and non-disruption of government supported programs and benefits, both of which are of primary concern for Linwood and Jordan.

As pertains to preservation of government benefits, if Julian directly owned the assets, he would not qualify for Supplemental Security Income Benefits referred to as SSI. In addition to providing him with a monthly stipend, SSI eligibility qualifies Julian for other governmental programs. Because Julian has no control over (does not own) the money or assets in a special needs trust, the contents of the trust are not considered when calculating Julian's total assets. The special needs trust thus ensures that Julian will remain eligible for governmental benefits and programs regardless of the actual value of his total assets.

There are three types of special needs trusts. The first type would be used by individuals providing for a special needs person. It is referred to as the third party funded trust. It is generally created by individuals like Linwood and Jordan in their will or in a living trust. Linwood and Jordan would use their own assets to fund this type of special needs trust.

The second type is a self-funded special needs trust set up for the disabled beneficiary. It is created with the assets or money of the disabled child. Generally, the disabled child's funds are derived from a personal injury settlement. For example, if Julian had been injured during birth due to negligence, then the proceeds from any settlement could be placed in the trust. In such a case, Julian's parent(s), as well as grandparent, guardian, or the courts, must create the trust. Under a self-funded special needs trust, any medical assistance payments received by Julian are required by law to be paid back. This is addressed by the terms in the trust, which is irrevocable.

The third type of special needs trust is the pooled trust. The trustee of a pooled trust must be a nonprofit fiduciary. Such trusts are generally established by non-profit organizations on behalf of their members. The trust provides the same benefits as standard special needs trusts. However, instead of benefitting an individual, the trust funds address the needs of all the members of the organization. For example, if

Julian lived in a group home for special needs individuals, the group home could establish a pooled trust that provides for all individuals within the home. Linwood and Jordan or others may contribute funds to the trust. The money placed in the pool, however, cannot be withdrawn and individual family members cannot direct how the funds will be used. The pooled funds continue to benefit other disabled individuals upon the death of the beneficiary.

In conclusion, the special needs trust will serve to protect Julian's assets and preserve his government benefits. As pertains to asset protection, Julian has never managed his financial affairs because he lacked the mental capacity. A special needs trust ensures that Julian's assets will remain under the control of an appointed trustee, who has a duty to protect Julian's assets and to act in Julian's best interest at all times. While the funds may not be given directly to Julian, they may be used to pay for his continued education, medical expenses, personal care attendants, or any other goods or services that benefit Julian. Additionally, the funds in the trust account are not subject to creditors or seizure. Thus, the funds will remain available to care for Julian at all times.

Marital Trusts

As Max and Margaret get close to retirement, they realize that their estate planning is due for updating. Fortunately, their financial portfolio has grown significantly. Max's stock options with Micro-Hard Technologies are worth several million dollars. Margaret's deferred compensation, along with the inheritance from her father, has made her a multi-millionaire as well. Together their estate exceeds the federal estate tax exclusion amount, which in 2009 is 3.5 million dollars.

For federal estate tax-planning purposes, marital trusts would be particularly important for Max and Margaret. They both, as well as all individuals, have a credit against any federal estate taxes due at death. However, this credit would be lost by the first spouse to die if a certain type of marital trust was not available. In order to protect or preserve the credit of the first spouse, such credit amount must be placed in a trust. The specific marital trust is often referred to as a credit shelter trust. It enables the surviving spouse to receive income during the surviving spouse's lifetime. In certain circumstances, the trustee can invade the principal for the benefit of the surviving spouse. The intent is that the remaining amount ultimately passes to the children or other beneficiaries tax free. Only with the use of this type of trust can the credit be preserved to pass tax free after the second spouse's death. Therefore, Max and Margaret's sons will inherit tax free the credit amount in the credit shelter trust at the same time that they receive, tax free, the credit of the second parent to die. This is a substantially huge tax benefit for the next generation.

In addition to the credit available against federal estate taxes to be paid, Max and Margaret can benefit from the marital deduction, which allows a spouse to transfer assets to the surviving spouse tax free. The funds can be left outright to the surviving spouse or in trust. Two important marital trusts are the qualified terminable interest Trust "QTIP" and qualified domestic trust "QDOT." Their use depends upon your circumstances.

The QTIP is generally considered when there is not only an interest in making sure that the surviving spouse is protected but also an interest in making sure that subsequent beneficiaries are covered. This would be of particular interest to those in a second marriage. After Max's divorce from his first wife, he married Margaret. If Max died before Margaret, the QTIP would allow Max to provide lifetime benefits to Margaret. It further serves as an assurance of an inheritance to all his children including his two sons from his first marriage. Without the QTIP, there is no guarantee that Margaret will provide for her stepsons. Further, if Margaret should remarry, any assets not in trust could become marital property available to her new husband. The terms and conditions of the QTIP can also provide for consistency in financial management if Margaret did not handle the financial affairs.

If the circumstances were different and Margaret was a non-U.S. citizen, the qualified domestic trust would have to be used to enable the marital deduction, which permits the transfer of assets without taxation to Margaret, the surviving spouse. The QDOT is the vehicle that allows a foreign or non-U.S. citizen spouse to benefit from the marital deduction or the tax free transfer of assets. Without funds being transferred into a QDOT, Margaret would have significant tax consequences. A U.S. citizen has to serve as the trustee for the QDOT. The primary purpose of this trust is to ensure that taxes are paid to the federal government when Margaret dies. The federal government could not reach these assets if Margaret should leave with the assets to another country.

Other Tax-Planning Trusts

Max and Margaret have other trust options available to them. Those include tax-planning trusts, such as the qualified personal residence trust, dynasty trust and irrevocable life insurance trust.

Qualified Personal Residence Trusts

A qualified personal residence trust "QPRT" can significantly reduce the overall tax costs of transferring a home to children or other beneficiaries while allowing you to continue to use the home to live in. You make a gift of your home to the trust for a period of years that you determine at the outset and during which time you retain the right to use it. If you survive the period, the home passes to the named beneficiary at a reduced tax-value rate.

The QPRT was created by Congress when concerns arose about inheritors of a house having to sell the real estate because they could not pay the taxes when ownership was transferred to them. Creating a QPRT of one's home or second home can significantly decrease taxes at the time that the residence is inherited since the value of the home is reduced based upon the number of years the property is held in the trust. After the term of years in the trust, what is left is the remainder interest in the residence.

In order to create this kind of trust, Max and Margaret transfer the house's title to the QPRT. The trust is created for the benefit of their sons and is owned by their sons. This transfer involves an agreement pertaining to the length of time Max and Margaret will continue to reside in the house. The intent is that while the house is in trust, Max and Margaret can still occupy it. Max's and Margaret's occupancy period reduces the total tax value of the gifted home for inheritance and estate tax purposes. Continued residency by Max and Margaret for a specified number of years is the primary feature of the QPRT.

To further elaborate, the QPRT allows the value of a gift of the house to be deferred so that the final tax value of the gift does not equal the true value of the actual house. In fact, the value will be much less because it is reduced by the number of years of occupancy by Max and Margaret as the owners. Therefore, when they no longer live in the home after the specified time period provided in the trust, their sons, as owners of the trust, are only liable in taxes for the value of the gift, not for the true value of the home. Since the home value will be reduced to the value of the gift, the need to sell the home to pay taxes is significantly reduced.

The QPRT trust has other specific guidelines or features, which may make choosing this type of trust either more or less attractive. If Max and Margaret die prior to the end of the term of occupancy, the home is considered part of Max's and Margaret's estate, whoever is the last to die. Their sons will not be able to claim the reduced value of the home and will be responsible for full taxes on the total value of the home.

Max and Margaret, as the owners and occupants of the house in the QPRT, are not able to claim any tax deductions associated with owning the house. They cannot mortgage or refinance the house, since they no longer own the property. Additionally, when the stated term of residence is up, technically they have to vacate the house to the new owners.

Of course, since the home is owned by their sons and not a charity, Max and Margaret may continue to rent or stay in the home free of charge. However, this right is not protected. For the QPRT to cause the least hassle, specific legal agreements, even with family members, should specify Max's and Margaret's legal right to stay in the home once the occupancy period is over. Further, the deferment period of ownership should be well considered. Though longer occupancy means the gift has less value, this can mean virtually nothing if Max and Margaret die before the term of occupancy is over.

However, the QPRT has some advantages. Since Max and Margaret no longer own the house, no fines, fees, or bills can be levied against the estate. This can serve to protect older individuals who might suffer a catastrophic illness and have huge hospital bills. The hospital cannot demand any money that might be achieved by refinancing or selling the house, since the occupant does not have any right to that money.

Dynasty Trusts

Max and Margaret can further plan for future generations through another tax-saving trust, the dynasty trust. The basic premise underlying the federal gift and estate tax system is that assets are subject to taxation each time they pass from one generation to another. Nonetheless, prior to 1986, these taxes were successfully avoided by many families through the use of "dynasty trusts" created for the benefit of successive generations of the descendants of the original donor or donors.

In 1986, in order to limit the tax-free or tax-advantageous transfer of wealth through dynasty trusts, Congress enacted the federal generation-skipping transfer "GST" tax. In its simplest application, the 1986 law taxes the assets held in a dynasty trust at the death of a trust beneficiary essentially as though the beneficiary owned the assets outright and as though the assets were included in the beneficiary's estate for purposes of the federal estate tax. However, Congress included a significant exemption in the GST tax law. Under the law, every person has a "GST exemption." As a result, Max and

Margaret could create and fund a dynasty trust with property having a value of up to $4,000,000, for married couples; the exemption is $2,000,000 for each individual. Within these limits, a dynasty trust can be created that has all the gift and estate-tax advantages of similar trusts created before 1986. Under IRS rules, a dynasty trust can allow trust assets to be managed for the benefit of Max's and Margaret's family for several generations. In essence, for Max and Margaret, a dynasty trust would be a long-term trust created for the benefit of their sons, grandchildren, and other descendants.

The tax savings associated with a dynasty trust do not occur when it is first funded. The tax savings occur later as the dynasty trust is administered for the benefit of Max's and Margaret's sons and other descendants. Once the original transfer of assets into the dynasty trust has occurred, the trust assets, as well as their appreciation and accumulated income, remain free from federal gift and estate taxes.

As with other trusts, the provisions of the trust can serve to protect and preserve the asset for the beneficiary only, Max's and Margaret's descendants. The trust can insulate the assets from the reach of the creditors of the descendants of Max and Margaret until, or unless, distributions are in fact made to the descendants, and it can prevent a spouse of any descendants from reaching any of the assets of the trust upon divorce for purposes of alimony or division of property. The dynasty trust illustrates a fundamental truth about estate planning: it is generally more beneficial for family wealth to be held in trust than to be owned outright by successive generations of family members.

Irrevocable Life Insurance Trusts

Another aspect to consider in estate planning for Max and Margaret is how much life insurance they have. Though proceeds from the life insurance policy are not taxable, the policy value is considered a part of the owner's estate for federal estate-tax purposes. Therefore, if Max or Margaret own life insurance, then they should look at ways to shift that ownership out of their estate. One way to accomplish that objective is through the use of an irrevocable life insurance trust "ILIT."

The ILIT is of particular benefit to those like Max and Margaret, who probably would have significant life insurance that is not needed for income purpose. If the insurance is only for the benefit of their sons, then it is best if the insurance policy is placed in an ILIT. If it is owned by the ILIT, it is not considered an asset of either Max's or Margaret's estate. It is best to have an ILIT actually purchase the insurance. However, if Max and Margaret already own insurance and want to transfer it to an ILIT, there will be a three-year look back period. This means that the person who creates the ILIT, Max or Margaret, will have to live beyond three years for the ILIT to be effective. If the creator of the ILIT, Max or Margaret, dies within the three-year period, the ILIT is not effective and the value of the insurance is considered an asset of the estate. Depending upon Max's and Margaret's circumstances, an ILIT can serve an important estate planning benefit.

The last two types of trusts mentioned in this section, pet trusts and charitable trusts, would be of particular benefit to Eve and Bob. As mentioned earlier, Eve and Bob breed show dogs and actively engage in charitable endeavors that specifically benefit dogs.

Pet Trusts

Pet trusts are more prevalent today. Many states, such as Pennsylvania, have established a pet trust law. Eve's and Bob's dogs, therefore, can serve as the actual beneficiary under the pet trust with a named trustee responsible for managing the asset for the benefit of the show dogs.

Even if Eve and Bob did not live in a state with a pet trust statute, they could still create a special trust for the benefit of their show dogs. The trust allows Eve and Bob to set aside money, either during their lifetime or upon their death, for the care and maintenance of their show dogs. Under this arrangement, Eve and Bob would choose a person who is willing to serve as caretaker for show dogs. This person would be the actual trust beneficiary (not the show dogs as in a pet trust) and would be entitled to distributions from the trust to pay for the show dog's expenses. Additionally, a final beneficiary should be chosen who would receive any assets still held by the trust upon the death of the show dogs. A trustee would also be chosen who would have the responsibility of making distributions of trust assets to the caretaker of the show dogs so long as the caretaker is satisfactorily caring for them.

In order to prevent their daughter, Julia, from contesting the validity of the trust, Eve and Bob should make sure that the amount of money used to fund the trust is not excessive. Otherwise, Julia, who may feel the show dogs are infringing upon her inheritance, could allege that the amount of money in the trust exceeds what is actually needed to provide care for the show dogs. If she can successfully demonstrate her allegation, the court will reduce the amount of money held by the trust. For these reasons, pet owners should proceed with caution and seek expert advice when setting up a pet trust in those states with statutes for pet trust or a trust that includes benefits for their pets.

Charitable Trusts

Eve and Bob can continue their charitable endeavors through the use of charitable trusts. During their lifetime, Eve and Bob have been motivated to support charities that benefit animals. Such charities have touched their life's passion. They can continue their support of their charities with various types of charitable trusts. The specific types of charitable trusts are covered in Chapter 13 on Charitable Estate Planning.

What is important to remember is that there are many types of trusts to address the myriad of circumstances that any individual may present during an estate planning review process.

Part 3:

The Journey of Your Estate

9: Intestate Law

In her thirties, Ria is developing an extremely profitable consulting business for herself. Her travels keep her constantly on the go, and she rarely has time to think beyond the day-to-day operation of her business. Though she has a five year and a ten year projection plan for the future of her business, she has not addressed the possibility of her incapacity or the eventuality of her death.

As has been discussed, Ria is not alone in this failure to plan. As a result, many people like Ria will be subject to the intestate laws of the state where they live.

What Does Intestate Mean?

Intestate means to die without a will. The intestate law represents the state's plan if Ria dies without a will. It is important to note that under many states' intestate law, including Pennsylvania's, Ria's estate does not go directly to the state. There is a succession of heirs entitled to Ria's estate, and they, including distant relatives, take precedent over the state.

Considering Ria's current situation, let's review Pennsylvania's intestate law:

Married Individuals - The spouse inherits entire estate unless one or more parent is living; then the spouse gets the first $30,000 and 1/2 of the balance. Remaining 1/2 goes to parent(s). At present Ria is not married, so we proceed to the next section of Pennsylvania's intestate law.

Married Individuals with Children - The spouse gets the first $30,000 and 1/2 the balance. Remaining 1/2 goes equally to children. However, if the deceased has children that are not from the current marriage, the spouse gets 1/2, and the remaining 1/2 is equally distributed to the children. This section as well does not apply to Ria.

Estate of Single Individuals - All is equally distributed to children; if there are no children, the following is the order of inheritance:

- parents
- brothers and sisters or their children
- grandparents
- uncles and aunts or their decedent's
- The Commonwealth of Pennsylvania

Based upon this section, Ria's parents would inherit her entire estate if Ria does not adopt a child. However, her parents' health has been rapidly failing. Both require some level of care. Fortunately, they can manage with in-home care. There is a potential, however, that they might need more extensive care. Under these circumstances, they would not have the ability to manage an inheritance. Furthermore, without proper planning, Ria's estate could be depleted by nursing home costs. With proper planning, Ria can address her parents' situation much more effectively.

What is the Purpose of the Intestate Law?

The intestate law represents a codification of the common law. The rules generally applied emerged from what may now be considered an outdated philosophy on the family and extended family structure. The state's plan is not a one-size-fits-all. It may meet the needs of some but, as with Ria, not meet the needs of everyone.

In essence, the purpose of the intestate laws is ease of administration. It does not and cannot address all of the possible interests, needs, and situations that could possibly exist for each and every individual.

This can only be addressed through the individualized process of estate planning. Ria can take control of the destiny of her assets through effective estate planning.

The issues that may arise if Ria fails to plan are many. If she adopts, who has rights to her estate? Adoption is established by state law, which considers an adopted child to be the child of the adoptive parent and therefore the child inherits from the adoptive parent, not the birth parent. Further, what happens to Ria's child? Which of Ria's relatives, if any, will become guardian of her child? Her sister Michele is busy with their ailing parents, and Ria is estranged from her brothers. Based upon these facts, how involved will the state become in determining her child's future? There could be many competing interests regarding her child, especially if money is involved. If there is disagreement among family members, the decision regarding guardianship may end up in the courts. Temporary arrangements for her child could last for months or longer. The death of a parent is significant enough for any child without the added uncertainty of who will now care for him or her. Ria can alleviate such a circumstance through planning.

Further, who will manage the distribution of Ria's estate upon her death? If she dies without a will, the court will have to appoint an administrator to handle her affairs. Since there is no executor (a person named under a will), the administrator is determined by law. Generally, the administrator is picked from among the beneficiaries or heirs. This would be Ria's parents, both of whom are unable to serve given their health condition. If Ria has a child, the child would be too young to serve. The court, in such a situation, could make an independent appointment.

Naming an Administrator of the Estate

If Ria dies without a will, the order of preference in the appointment of an administrator under Pennsylvania intestate law is as follows:

(1)   the surviving spouse

(2)   those entitled to the estate under the intestate law given preference to those with the significant share of the estate

(3)   the principal creditors of the decedent

(4)   other fit persons as may be determined by the courts

Those considered eligible to serve as administrator can decide among themselves the most appropriate one or ones to serve, and the court will make the appointment based upon the recommendation of the heirs. If no one that is entitled to serve is willing or able to serve, or if there are disputes among the heirs, the courts will make an appointment. The more details that can be worked out among heirs, the less involvement required by the court.

A court-appointed administrator is entitled to compensation for services as administrator. The compensation is paid from Ria's estate. Under a will, Ria can determine whether or not her executor will be compensated and how much. Reimbursement from the estate for expenses incurred is generally understood and permitted whether or not addressed by the will. Of course, it is best for Ria to be as specific as possible in her will regarding any financial entitlements.

Bond Requirements of An Administrator

In addition, under a will Ria can address whether the person who manages the distribution of her estate must post a bond. Generally, it is specifically provided in a will that the executor does not have to post a bond. If it is not specified or there is no will, the court can require a bond. A bond (if not otherwise provided for in the will) is generally required if the person lives out of state. The bond protects the court and the assets of the estate.

Spouse's Elective Share Rule

Let's reflect back to Julia, Eve's and Bob's daughter who had two broken marriage engagements. Well, now Julia is married, but things are not working out as she had hoped. However, she does not want to file for divorce, but she does want to make sure her husband does not inherit any of her money if she predeceases him. Since Julia is married, no matter what her intent is regarding a divorce, if she chooses to disinherit her husband (not provide for her husband in her will), her will would not supersede her husband's legal rights. If Julia lives in Pennsylvania when she dies, no matter what her will provides, her husband is entitled to 1/3 of her estate. This legal right is known as the elective share rule. The public policy behind the elective share rule is to prevent one spouse from disinheriting the other. It assures that the surviving spouse will at least have a minimal share of the decedent's estate.

The assets over which Julia's husband has the right to make the election include property passing upon Julia's death, by her will or by intestacy, dying without a will. In addition, assets conveyed during marriage, by Julia to herself and another with rights of survivorships, are also included in her estate subject to her husband's elective right. Finally, assets that were given away by Julia within one year of death, to the extent that the gift exceeded $3,000, are subject to her husband's elective right.

The elective share rule is an election that Julia's husband must affirmatively make in order to receive the 1/3 share. The request for election must be filed no later than six months after Julia's death. This legal right can be lost if Julia's husband forfeits his right by deserting Julia's during her lifetime. Also, the use of a prenuptial agreement may eliminate the possibility of Julia's husband electing against her will. However, if Julia was separated at the time of her death, her husband is still entitled to his elective share. He is her husband until such time as a divorce is finalized.

Another option available to Julia's husband is to seek to have the will declared invalid. In such a case, Julia's estate is treated as though there was no will. His challenge can be made regarding adherence to the statutory requirements for making a will. This includes whether it was properly executed and whether Julia was of sound mind at the time of execution. That is why it is important that Julia address all aspects of her life as part of her estate plan. Obtaining professional expertise is essential for her to accomplish her goals.

distributions to the beneficiaries are made. That is why a notification to creditors must be provided in legal publications. In Pennsylvania, notification to creditors is satisfied by placing an advertisement in the papers that provides Linwood's name and address as executor. The advertisement runs for three successive weeks. Linwood is not liable to any unknown creditors after this legal notification period. Even though distributions can be made prior to the end of the notification, Linwood is at risk if the notification period has not lapsed. Since the debts of Jordan must be satisfied, Linwood would become liable for such debt. The notification period serves to protect Linwood from liability in this regard.

Next, Linwood, as executor is required to provide notification to those entitled to Jordan's assets. He is also responsible for the inheritance tax return, which is due within nine months of Jordan's death. Linwood can pay the tax from the estate or reduce the amount due the beneficiary by the amount of the tax due. Jordan may have addressed this issue in the will. If the will is silent or there is no will, the tax is still due. Linwood must determine the best method to assure payment of the taxes. Even though the tax authorities could and may proceed against the individuals who inherit, it would be prudent for Linwood to make sure payments are made to avoid personal liability.

As discussed in Chapter 9 under Bond Requirements of an Administrator, it is important that the will address the issue of bond or surety. If Jordan's will was silent on this issue or there is no will, the register of wills could require Linwood to post a bond or surety. Generally, the register of wills would require such a filing if the fiduciary, Linwood, lived out-of-state. This is because there is less control over an out-of-state fiduciary if such fiduciary should fail to comply with the statutory duties of the state.

Role of Probate Court

Though the register of wills can probate an estate without court involvement, litigation is sometimes unavoidable. There are potential issues for Linwood whether or not Jordan had a will. If Jordan's heirs are not satisfied with the terms of the will which did not provide for them, they could contest it. The legitimate bases of a will contest include questions regarding Jordan's competency. Was Jordan of sound mind? Was Jordan under undue distress at the time of execution of the will? Were all of the legal requirements met for execution of the will? Was it in writing and signed by Jordan?

Jordan can (and did) disinherit family members. This decision by Jordan can lead to a challenge by such family members. The court will then have to determine whether all of the legal requirements for making a will are satisfied and whether there was any oversight in the exclusion of a potential heir. To avoid a successful challenge to the will, Jordan's intent must be clear.

A more complex issue would arise for Linwood if Jordan did not have a will. Linwood is not an heir or family member and, therefore, would not be entitled to any of the probate estate.

Probate and Non-Probate Assets

However, Linwood and Jordan could have avoided this potentiality by making sure that there were no "probate assets" at death, only "non-probate assets." "Non-probate assets" are those assets not subject to the probate process. They include the proceeds from life insurance policies and investment products (like annuities) where Jordan or Linwood named each other as the designated beneficiary. Jordan and Linwood could own assets jointly with rights of survivorship automatically passing to the other owner. Finally, assets not owned by Jordan or Linwood will not be subject to probate. As discussed earlier, this pertains to property either could have placed in a trust.

If Jordan does not own anything or does not have "probate assets," then there is no requirement to open an estate. However, Linwood's ability to avoid the probate process or not does not alleviate the payment of inheritance tax.

A Final Consideration

Finally, if there is no will, the heirs can open up the estate for distribution upon presentation of a death certificate. Proof of status as heirs is required. Distribution would be in accordance with the intestate laws which would not cover Linwood who is not an heir under those laws. If there is a controversy or a dispute, it will be necessary for intervention through the courts.

11: State Inheritance Taxes

Not all states have an inheritance tax, a tax upon death. Pennsylvania does have such a tax. Linwood, as executor of Jordan's estate or as beneficiary of Jordan's estate, will have to pay inheritance tax. Jordan's will may have indicated whether the estate assets would be used to pay any inheritance tax. If not, Linwood can determine payment responsibility. In either situation, it remains the responsibility of Linwood as executor to file the inheritance tax returns for the estate.

Tax Rates

The tax rates in Pennsylvania are as follows:

- Tax free surviving spouse, charity, transferred from a deceased child under 21 to parents or grandparents

- 4.5% grandparents, parents, children and their spouses, grandchildren and their spouses, stepchildren and their spouses, adopted children and their spouses

- 12% siblings

- 15% all others

Since Linwood does not fall in the first three categories, a 15% inheritance tax will have to be paid on Linwood's inheritance.

Filing an Inheritance Tax Return

Linwood has to file the inheritance tax return within nine months of Jordan's death. An extension may be requested. Within three months of Jordan's death, an estimated return can be filed.

The estate will be entitled to a discount for the early filing of an estimated return. Linwood does not want to overpay when doing the estimated return because even though a refund will be obtained, it will not include any interest.

A refund can be obtained for an overpayment as well as for a successful challenge to the tax amount. The challenge can be based upon a reassessment of the value of Jordan's estate.

Specifically, Jordan's assets are valued at the time of death based upon market value. Depreciation is taken into consideration. The tax imposed can be appealed to the Tax Revenue Board, but there must be an appealable issue to present.

With the exception of life insurance proceeds, tenancy by the entireties, and joint tenants with rights of survivorship, an inheritance tax is imposed on all other assets. This includes assets that Jordan may have placed in a trust for distribution to Linwood.

Disclaimer

Linwood can choose to disclaim (refuse to accept) any inheritance from Jordan. Linwood is then treated as having predeceased Jordan. Linwood must disclaim within nine months and reap no benefits of the property disclaimed. There are a number of reasons that Linwood may want to disclaim an inheritance, including tax planning purposes and avoidance of creditors. Your estate planning professional can help you determine when a disclaimer is applicable to your circumstances.

12: Federal Inheritance Tax

In many states, a state inheritance tax return is required. There is also an inheritance tax requirement on the federal level. The executor or administrator is responsible for filing both the state inheritance tax return, in states where required, and the federal inheritance tax return, if the estate is subject to the tax. Payment may come from the estate's assets, which is preferable, or from the inheritance of the beneficiaries. Any fiduciary for the estate has filing responsibility. This not only includes the executor or administrator but also a trustee if a trust has been established.

Tax Relief Act

The Tax Relief Act of 2001 significantly revised the federal estate tax law. It increased the lifetime exclusion, which represents the amount that can be left to heirs free of estate tax. In 2009 the lifetime exclusion amount is $3.5 million with the federal estate tax rate at 45%. The Tax Relief Act of 2001 has an interesting "sunset" provision that makes the entire law expire on December 31, 2010. Unless a new law is enacted by December 31, 2010, the estate tax law will revert to that which was in existence prior to the Tax Relief Act of 2001.

Lifetime Exclusion

Year of Death	Estate Tax Life-time Exclusion	Unified Tax Credit	Estate Tax Rates
2009	$3.5 Million	$1,455,800	45%
2010	Unlimited (Tax Repealed)	-	-

Given the significance of the federal estate tax, the need for tax planning to preserve the estate is crucial.

If Jordan dies in 2009 with an estate valued in excess of 3.5 million dollars, then the federal estate tax is applicable. The tax is calculated by determining the tax due on the entire estate, less applicable expenses and debts, without considering the lifetime exclusion amount. Assume Jordan's estate, less applicable expenses, debts and other allowable deductions, is 5 million dollars. At a 45% tax rate, the gross tax would be $2,250,000. An amount known as the unified tax credit ($1,455,800) is subtracted from the gross tax. The net amount of $794,200 represents the tax due from Jordan's estate. The unified tax credit reduces the gross tax dollar-for-dollar. The estate tax is due within nine months of Jordan's death.

Inventory and Value of Gross Estate

Before the federal estate tax can be determined, a careful inventory of all the assets that are included in Jordan's gross estate must be made. The value of the gross estate is then determined. This is necessary because the federal estate tax is based upon the fair market value of assets owned by Jordan. This value is determined as of the date of Jordan's death. The gross estate consists of real estate, bank accounts, financial assets, money loaned to others, business assets, closely held businesses, personal property, retirement plans, annuities, life insurance, and jointly owned assets. Though life insurance proceeds go tax free to the recipient beneficiary, if Jordan owns the policy, the insurance amount is part of the value of Jordan's estate.

Everyone has a lifetime exclusion amount. This is the amount that can pass free of federal estate tax at death. A husband and wife each has his or her own lifetime exclusion amount, which allows them to double the amount passing tax free to their heirs. However, if no prior tax planning is done, married taxpayers could lose the benefit of the credit of the first spouse to die, which otherwise can be preserved through the use of the credit shelter trust provided in the will or living trust as detailed in Chapter 8.

Deductions

Once the gross estate is identified and valued, a number of deductions are permitted. This includes the following:

- Debts and unpaid mortgages of the decedent
- Estate settlement expenses
- Charitable deduction
- Marital deduction

The marital deduction is only available to married couples. The surviving spouse must also be a U.S. citizen. If the surviving spouse is other than a U.S. citizen, a special type of trust must be used as a marital trust. This trust is known as a qualified domestic trust or "QDOT" as more fully discussed in Chapter 8. At least one trustee of the QDOT must be a citizen of the U.S. or a domestic corporation.

Gift Tax Law

The Tax Relief Act of 2001 also revised the gift tax law. However, there is no provision in the law that repeals what has been established regarding gift tax. Whenever assets are given to another for less than its full value, the amount by which the asset's value exceeds the money paid for them is a gift. Everyone has a lifetime gift exclusion amount of $1,000,000. As long as you do not gift over $1,000,000 during your lifetime, there will be no gift tax due. However, there is a gift tax filing required if you gift over a certain amount annually.

This annual exclusion amount for 2009 is $13,000, adjusted for inflation. The first $13,000 a donor gives to any single donee in any calendar year is excluded from the gift tax filing. Therefore, to the extent that in any given year Jordan gave $13,000 or less to any one person, there is no gift tax filing required. Gifts made to anyone, regardless of the relationship, qualify for this annual exclusion amount of $13,000.

Part 4:

Giving and Living Longer

13: Charitable Estate Planning

O ver the next few decades, it is estimated that trillions of dollars will be transferred from the parents of baby boomers to their children. Charitable giving will play an enormous role in this transfer of wealth. Although charitable giving provides many personal and tax benefits, it has a more fundamental benefit, which is voluntary giving. In contrast, involuntary giving is the result of overpayment of taxes. With proper planning, involuntary giving can be avoided. Individuals can voluntarily give money from their estate to the charities they desire.

Many people during their lifetime engage in charitable giving activities. They make gifts to cancer research, heart associations, educational institutions, or well water projects. Many give to hospitals, churches, or other religious and cultural institutions. Others have long term relationships with charities and want to continue charitable giving upon their death. Some, like Max and Margaret, have developed lifetime passions upon which they can create a legacy. Max collects historical manuscripts and other memorabilia on the American Revolution, and he wants his collection from this period of American life to serve many generations after his death. Without proper planning, his collection could languish in the attic or basement of his family homestead, or worst, be destroyed by those who may not understand the value.

Margaret's lifetime philanthropy has made a difference in the lives of many in her community, and she hopes that the foundation she helped to form continues to thrive after her death. As a result, both Max and Margaret want to know what charitable planning techniques would work best for their interest.

Charitable Bequests

There are many ways to engage in charitable estate planning. One of the most basic ways to make a charitable gift is through a bequest, which Max and Margaret could make in their wills or trusts. A bequest is appealing to Max and Margaret because they maintain control of their assets until they die, it is the easiest way to give, and it can also be changed at any time. The bequest is a statement in the will or trust identifying assets Max and Margaret want to leave and to which charitable institution they want to leave the assets.

Charitable Trusts

Max and Margaret should also consider the use of charitable trusts because these trusts have significant tax benefits. There are several charitable trusts to consider, such as the Charitable Remainder Annuity Trust (CRAT), Charitable Reminder Unitrust (CRUT) and Charitable Leads Trust. The first two trusts, CRAT and CRUT, permit Max and Margaret to provide a remainder interest to a charitable organization while they continue to benefit during their lifetime from the asset to be transferred. These trusts are considered split interest trusts. They have both charitable and non-charitable beneficiaries.

The Charitable Leads Trust is also a split interest trust. However, it is the reverse of the CRAT and CRUT. The Charitable Leads Trust pays income first to the charity for a term of years and then the remainder amount is paid back to Max or Margaret or, if the trust is established after their death, to their beneficiaries. This means that the charity gets paid first and then the non-charitable recipient. Therefore, the charity leads the non-charitable recipient. That is why this particular trust is referred to as a Charitable Leads Trust. The use of CRAT, CRUT and Charitable Leads Trust can offer financial advantages to Max and Margaret during their lifetime.

With the CRAT and CRUT, Max and Margaret, as the non-charitable beneficiary, have the right to receive, at least annually, an annuity or unitrust amount for life or for a term of years (not more than 20 years). At the end of the established term, the remaining assets of the trust are paid to or held for the benefit of charity. If the interest is an annuity interest, then the trust is considered a CRAT. When it is established, Max and Margaret choose the payout rate. The higher the payment to them, the lower the charitable deduction will be for tax purposes. If the interest is a unitrust interest, the trust is considered a CRUT. In the CRUT, the assets are revalued every year to determine the payout rate each year.

Whether Max and Margaret use a CRAT, CRUT, or a Charitable Leads Trust, they should choose appreciating assets to give and place in the trust. Since charities are not taxed, this will avoid a capital gain tax when the asset is sold by the charity. Therefore, for appreciating assets like real estate and stock, Max and Margaret get a charitable deduction during their lifetime and the charity avoids a capital gain tax.

Charitable Deduction

The amount of charitable deduction that Max and Margaret may be entitled to take in any one year is limited to a percentage of their adjusted gross income. The percentage is based upon the type of asset contributed and the type of charitable organizations to which their donation is made. Deduction for contributions of cash to public charities is limited to 50% of their adjusted gross income. Deduction contributions of appreciated capital gain property (i.e. real estate and stock) to public charities is limited to 30% of their adjusted gross income. If their charity is a private foundation, deduction for contributions of cash is 30% and for appreciated capital gain property, the deduction is 20% of their adjusted gross income.

What is a Qualified Charity?

Any organization Max and Margaret consider for charitable giving must meet certain criteria. A charity which qualifies for charitable gifts is one that is a charitable organization as described in the Internal

Revenue Code 501(c)(3). All nonprofit organizations are defined by the IRS as either "public charities" or "private foundation." **Public charities** include churches, schools, museum, hospitals, and medical research organizations. All public charities rely on public support. Contributions to a public charity would allow Max and Margaret to obtain an income tax deduction. As previously stated, the income tax deduction for cash contributions would be 50% of Max's and Margaret's adjusted gross income. For appreciated capital gain property contributions, there would be an income tax deduction of 30% of their adjusted gross income.

Private foundations are often founded by an individual or corporation and do not receive support from the public. Income tax deductions for contribution to a private foundation would be available to Max and Margaret but at a lesser amount. Again, as previously stated, the deduction for contributions of cash is 30% and for appreciated capital gain property, the deduction is 20% of their adjusted gross income.

Therefore, the private foundation is essentially a private tax exempt organization with the purpose of benefitting public charities, including educational institutions, research organizations, or other nonprofit organizations serving the public interest. A private foundation does not provide charitable services but makes grants to provide funding to other qualified charities. It is created and controlled by a single source of funds (usually a company or one individual or family) and not the general public. Private foundations are established by those who want a greater degree of control over administration, making grants, and investment of the assets donated to the private foundation than is possible with public charities.

Further, a private foundation of an individual or family can serve to transfer assets to the next generation. This is accomplished by involving the younger generation in the foundation's administration, management, and grant making. Children can learn about and engage in philanthropy at an early age.

The governing form of a private foundation can be either a trust or a nonprofit corporation. Once the organization has been established and the Board of Directors or trustees appointed, the IRS requires additional documentation. Private foundations must annually make a minimum distribution of their net investment assets to qualified public charities each year. Establishing a foundation and complying with its reporting requirements does incur ongoing legal and accounting expenses. When a private foundation is established by a family, all of the family members' charitable giving can be channeled into one vehicle, resulting in larger gifts and greater impact on their chosen charities.

There are also **community foundations**, which are classified by the IRS as public charities. They are organized as a permanent collection of endowed funds and charitable donations for the advantage of a defined geographic area. Establishing a fund or an account at a community foundation that permits such an arrangement achieves many of the same charitable objectives as a private foundation but without the same level of costs to administer.

The managing or governing body of a community foundation is made up of representatives of the general community. Like private foundations, they operate primarily as grant-making organizations. They accept gifts of cash and other tangible and intangible assets. Grants are made from specific funds of the community foundation in accordance with the established terms of the community foundation. Generally, community foundations have at least three different types of funds:

The Unrestricted Fund: This represents the discretionary fund of the community foundation. Distribution can be made at the complete discretion of the foundation.

The Restricted Fund: This represents the special interest fund of the community foundation. The special interest can be in areas such as the environment, arts, education, or health. The community foundation makes discretionary grants to other charities serving these fields of interest.

The Donor-Advised Fund: The donor may make specific recommendations or suggestions that potential grants are made to its preferred charity from funds given by the donor. Therefore, a donor-advised fund at a community foundation serves as an alternative to a donor setting up a private foundation. The donor comes under the tax and accounting umbrella of a public charity. Donors who want to be actively involved in grant making may designate this type of fund. The donor is an adviser, but the community foundation has final authority as to whether any recommendation is approved.

Max and Margaret should determine what charitable organization addresses their specific interest. For Max, it is important that his memorabilia from the American Revolution is available to use for scholarly research. The charitable organization that he chooses must have the capacity to meet his intentions. If not, Max could provide a monetary contribution in addition to his collection to assure its proper care and use. This endowment approach could also be used by Max during his lifetime to form his own charitable organization.

Margaret helped to establish a community foundation that she wants to continue to flourish upon her death. Similar to Max, she can create an endowment. She can provide a financial (monetary) gift to her foundation. The gift will serve as the principal for growth and income that would be used to fulfill Margaret's designated purpose. With proper investment oversight, her financial gift is lasting. For both Max and Margaret, their gifts help create their specific legacy by carrying on the missions reflective of their life.

Max and Margaret realize that it is to their advantage to make their gifts during their lifetime. They get an income tax deduction for their gifts, avoid a capital gains tax on their gift of significantly appreciated stock, and just as important, they reduce the value of their estate. They have removed valuable assets from their estate so those assets will not be taxable to their estate upon their death.

For these and other charitable donations that Max and Margaret may make, they must make sure to maintain adequate records. Regardless of the amount of a monetary contribution, they must substantiate that it was made. This can be done by retaining the canceled check, bank record, or the written communication for the charitable organization that shows their name, the date, and the amount of contribution.

14: As We Age - Elder Law Issues

Introduction

In the expansive auditorium, hundreds of freshman college students sat silently listening to the president of the university give his welcome address. As Mary recalls, it was filled with all the requisite statements of hope and promises of bright and prosperous futures. He instructed each student to look first to the left and then to the right. As everyone complied, he told them that they would make many lasting friends and new acquaintances who would make their matriculation there memorable. She smiled pleasantly at her roommate who sat on her left.

Mary looked to her right and her heart beat accelerated and her breath stilled. Her eyes connected with his in that instant. It was as though time took a brief holiday, and only the two of them existed for that moment. To this day, over 40 years later, his smile holds her heart captive. Mary and Charles have shared a life together filled with love and cherished memories, from the birth of their only son Jack to the birth of their three beautiful granddaughters.

Initially, Charles' lapses in memory seemed innocuous to Mary. He might forget a person's name, neglect to pick up items from the store, or misplace his car keys. Subsequently, his business partner started to raise questions regarding Charles' forgetfulness. He noticed Charles had difficulty in focusing and organizing his thoughts, some-times redoing completed projects. Mary then stopped disregarding the hints of medical illness. However, by that time, they were already near financial ruin.

Mary and Charles are coping with the most significant physical, emotional, and financial crisis of their lives. Charles has been diag-nosed with Alzheimer's, the most devastating form of dementia. It is irreversible and progressive and robs millions of older Americans like Charles of their use of language, reasoning, memory, and judgment. It further irrevocably alters the lives of families.

Mary has found it necessary to redefine their relationship as husband and wife. Though she has worked, Charles handled all of their financial affairs. Now, she has to not only become financially astute but also address the financial crisis they face. Alzheimer's is the third most costly disease after heart disease and cancer, and it has taken a significant financial and emotional toll on them.

As Charles' primary caregiver, Mary must take off many hours and days from work to fulfill her caregiving role. Charles has only minor physical ailments; therefore, Mary cares for him at home. However, Mary realizes that she needs additional help for her to continue to work which is needed now more than ever. What options are available to address the cost of home-care? Are assisted living facility or other extended care options available to Charles? How can Mary address these long-term care costs for Charles? These are among the issues Mary presents to her attorney.

Elder Law

In the area of estate planning, issues of particular interest to an aging population often emerge. The increasing dynamics of this population demand not only traditional estate planning but also more focus on healthcare and long-term care planning. With this shift in emphasis, the practice of elder law has become recognized as a distinct legal discipline. It would take another book to address the full spectrum of this area of practice. This chapter only addresses the important healthcare and long-term care needs, which serve as focus areas for elder law. Therefore, Mary's and Charles' situation will be addressed in the context of social security and long-term care insurance.

The social security areas covered include retirement, disability, Medicare and Medicaid. In addition, this chapter concludes with the topic of guardianship since incapacity is another issue our society is facing more and more.

Social Security

Social security is multifaceted. It is much more than just a retirement program. Even though most social security participants receive their payments as retired workers, there are a wide variety of programs under social security. These programs are vital to the lives of seniors as well as many younger individuals. Throughout the history of social security, significant programs have been established. The programs that will be addressed in this chapter include

- Retirement Insurance
- Disability Insurance
- Supplemental Security Income
- Medicare
- Medicaid (Medical Assistance)

Each of these benefit programs has specific eligibility criteria that must be met to receive the specific benefit. Let's determine which ones benefit Charles and Mary.

Retirement Insurance

Charles and Mary are both 58 years old and have worked since graduating from their alma mater. Both are eligible to retire with benefits from their current employment. Charles has retired because of his disability, but Mary continues to work to meet their increasing medical needs. She is looking into social security benefits that may be available to Charles now.

However, neither Charles nor Mary qualifies for social security retirement benefits. Under the social security laws, they would only be eligible for retirement benefits if they were at least age 62 and had paid into social security for the requisite period. For most people, this would be at least ten years of full-time work.

Further, Charles' and Mary's benefit payment would be based on how much they earned during their working career. Higher lifetime earnings result in higher benefits. If there were some years when they did not work or had low earnings, their benefit amount would be lower than if they had worked steadily.

The full retirement age is 65 for people who were born before 1938. But because of longer life expectancies, the social security law was changed to gradually increase the full retirement age until it reaches age 67. This change affects people born in 1938 and later. Charles and Mary were born in 1950, and their full retirement age will be 66.

Mary and Charles, like many other retirees, could choose to receive their social security benefits before they attain their full retirement age. If they begin to receive social security retirement benefits before full retirement age, their monthly payments will be reduced. Once the full retirement age is 67, the permanent reduction for a worker retiring at age 62 will be 30 percent. Nevertheless, there are many retirees who choose to take benefits as soon as possible at age 62 due solely to the fear that social security is not secure and that benefits may be reduced in the future.

An important fact to remember is that social security is intended to supplement, not replace, the total financial resources needed by a worker at retirement. Social security retirement benefits replace about 40 percent of an average wage earner's income, less if the benefit is permanently reduced due to early retirement. The belief is that at retirement age, your financial needs are reduced. The mortgage on your home is paid off or you downsize to a smaller home. Your children have left home and are independent or possibly providing assistance to you. You have no long-term healthcare needs. Is this the reality for most retirees? Many financial planners suggest that 70–80 percent of an average wage earner's income will be needed for a comfortable retirement. Our changed reality demands more advance planning for retirement than most people have realized.

Disability Insurance

Based on the foregoing section, Charles is not eligible for social security retirement benefits. However, he may obtain disability insurance from one of the two social security programs that cover disability. They are the Social Security Disability Insurance (SSDI) program and the Supplemental Security Income (SSI) program.

The SSDI program provides benefits to workers who are disabled and their spouses and children. SSDI payments only partially replace the earnings of a worker who has become permanently unable to engage in substantial gainful activity. These benefits are paid to the disabled worker and to the worker's dependent family members.

To be eligible for SSDI, Charles must show that he has an impairment that has lasted or is expected to last 12 months or result in death, and is so severe that it prevents him from engaging in substantial gainful activity. In addition, he must have an employment history of work covered by social security. In Charles' case, he was diagnosed with Alzheimer's over two years ago. At that time, he could no longer work. He had worked the requisite period of time to make him eligible for the disability insurance coverage.

The amount of Charles' disability benefit is usually the same as full retirement benefit. Charles' SSDI benefits will be converted to retirement benefits when he attains full retirement age.

The other disability insurance program is Supplemental Security Income (SSI). It is a federal income supplement program administered by social security but funded by general tax revenues and not social security taxes. SSI is designed to help the elderly and disabled, who have little or no income, by providing money to meet basic needs for food, clothing, and shelter. In effect, SSI serves to ensure that elderly and disabled people have a minimum level of income if they do not qualify for social security or if their social security benefits are too low.

In order to receive SSI benefits, Charles' monthly income must be low, under a specified amount as determined by law and subject to annual increases based on cost-of-living adjustments. Charles' pension and savings would provide too much income and/or resources for him to qualify. Mary's income would also affect eligibility. Therefore, Charles' option for disability insurance would be SSDI and not SSI.

Medicare

Medicare is another benefit available to individuals who have paid into the social security system. It is an entitlement at age 65 and is not based upon income and assets. Certain people younger than age 65, like Charles, can qualify for Medicare. In Charles' specific case, this would include persons under 65 who have been eligible for SSDI or SSI for at least 24 months. Medicare can help with the cost of Charles' healthcare, but it does not cover all medical expenses or the cost of most long-term care. Let's first review what medical expenses are covered under the program. We can then determine what other options and alternatives may be available for Charles' situation.

Historically, the Medicare program was composed of two parts. Medicare Part A is often referred to as Hospital Insurance (HI). However, it does provide some non-hospital benefits. Medicare Part B is also known as Supplementary Medical Insurance (SMI).

As the needs of our society have evolved, additional parts have been added to Medicare. Medicare Part C was added to expand the managed care options for Medicare beneficiaries. Managed care options were already being provided by some private industries. Later, Medicare Part D was added. It provided access to drug insurance coverage on a voluntary basis for all beneficiaries and prescription premium and cost sharing subsidies for low income individuals.

Medicare Parts A, B, and D cover various healthcare services and prescription drugs. Part C provides no additional healthcare services but offers an alternate, more privatized, means of delivery of hospital and medical benefits. An individual can choose to enroll in either Parts A or B or in Part C. With the combination of the different Parts, individuals receive assistance for the following:

- hospital inpatient care, nursing home care for a limited period of time following hospital inpatient care, home-care, and hospice-care (Part A) (deductibles and copayments applicable);

- doctor services, outpatient medical care and supplies at a hospital, some home-care, ambulance, physical and speech therapy, and durable medical equipment (Part B) (premiums, deductibles and copayments applicable);

- managed care – Medicare Advantage Plans (Part C) (premiums, deductibles and copayments applicable); and

- prescription drugs coverage for medications doctors prescribe for treatment (Part D) (premiums, deductibles and copayments).

However, there is no coverage under the Medicare program for the following:

- custodial care in a nursing home;

- dental care and dentures;

- some routine checkups and tests directly related to these checkups;

- most immunization shots;

- routine foot care; and

- tests for, and the cost of, eyeglasses or hearing aids.

The Medicare program is not a comprehensive health program. Some health services are not covered and those that are require that individuals stay knowledgeable of changes in benefits and costs. For example, individuals are responsible for deductibles, copayments, and premiums. Due to gaps in the services covered under Medicare, many individuals keep their private insurance plan or, if applicable, an employer provided group health plan. In addition, some purchase a Medicare supplement (Medigap) insurance policy or seek more comprehensive or lower cost coverage through a Medicare Managed Care Part C option.

As pertains to Medigap, many private insurers sell insurance to fill in the gaps in Medicare. Medigap policies may pay most or all Medicare copayment amounts and, in some cases, may provide for Medicare deductibles. Some of the policies even pay for services not covered by Medicare at all.

Further, in order to address gaps in the traditional Medicare coverage (Part A and B), individuals, like Charles, may opt to enroll in a managed care program, Part C. There are a number of different forms of Medicare Advantage Plans: Medicare Managed Care Plans, Medicare Preferred Provider Organization Plans (PPO), Medicare Private Fee-for Service Plans, and Medicare Specialty Plans. There are many factors that individuals, like Mary on Charles' behalf, need to consider in their healthcare decision making process. Are your doctors covered under certain plans? Having access to your doctors and certain hospitals is of importance to many people. What extra benefits do you need? The supplemental benefits offered under Part C vary widely and may even change each year. Charles' situation is very specific, and Mary will want to make sure any plan covers their essential needs. What are the costs, deductibles, and copayment requirements? Affordability is a key consideration for Mary. What is the quality and reputation of any chosen plan? Review and research is critical for Mary and should be for anyone in making a final decision to enroll.

A final important consideration for Mary as she reviews Medicare is the prescription drug program (Part D). Charles does take medication for his Alzheimer's and, in the future, will have other prescription drug needs. There are two types of plans for Medicare drug coverage:

- Medicare prescription drug plan that only covers prescription drugs and no other benefits, paired with the traditional Medicare program (Part A and B); or

- Managed care plan (Medicare Advantage Plan) which covers Medicare benefits, including prescription drugs.

The Medicare drug benefit is voluntary. If an individual already has a generous source of drug coverage, such as under retirement benefits, that coverage may be more beneficial. The need to sign up for a Medicare prescription drug plan or the Medicare Advantage Plan is alleviated.

Charles does qualify for Medicare because of his qualification for SSDI. As discussed, the Medicare hospital coverage is free, but there is a monthly premium for medical insurance. Since Mary is covered under the health insurance Charles maintains as a retiree with his former employer, she determines Medicare medical insurance is not worth the additional monthly premium that Charles would incur. It may be something for Mary to consider at a later time, but their private insurer arrangement has been working for her and Charles. This includes the coverage now available to them for Charles' prescription drugs.

However, what concerns Mary the most is the prospect of Charles' long-term care needs given their current financial limitations. At present, Charles' physical ailments are minimal. However, Mary realizes there will be ongoing mental as well as physical erosion. She may want to or have to change their current health insurance arrangement in the future, so it is best that she continues to explore her future options.

If Charles qualifies, Medicare will cover home health benefits. He would be entitled to Medicare coverage of his home health care if he meets the following requirements:

- He is confined to his home (meaning that leaving it to receive services would be a "considerable and taxing effort" for Charles).

- His doctor has ordered home health services for him.

- At least some element of the services he receives is skilled (some skilled nursing care, physical therapy, or speech therapy).

If Mary has to consider a nursing home for Charles' care, there would be limited payments under Medicare. Specifically, Medicare Part A covers only up to 100 days of care in a nursing home. The care in the nursing home must follow an admission in a hospital. There is a copayment for some of the days in the nursing home. The definition of skilled nursing and the other conditions for obtaining Medicare coverage are quite stringent and must be met in order to receive the full 100 days for coverage.

Mary realizes that if Charles should require skilled nursing in the future, she will have to make sure that Charles gets his full benefit. She is advised that typically, after a certain amount of time in a skilled nursing facility, she, as Charles' wife, will be informed in writing that Charles is no longer making progress with physical therapy or other skilled treatment and that Medicare coverage will end. However, any success from the treatment, even if it simply slows down deterioration, supports continuation of the treatment and of the Medicare coverage. In such a situation, Mary must advocate for continued physical or other therapy for Charles, due to the benefit of the treatment, and to extend Medicare coverage.

If the termination of coverage remains a threat, Mary can exercise her option, as provided in the written notice, to ask for a review. There's no cost to Mary for the review, so there's no reason for her not to request it. During the review process, Charles does not have to pay for his care. However, if the termination of benefits is upheld, Charles will be responsible for the cost of care back to the date of the termination notice.

Even if the outcome of the review is favorable to Charles, there is only 100 total days of coverage. Charles has longer term care needs. Since neither Medicare nor private health insurance provides long-term care, Mary has to determine how Charles's long-term care expenses will be paid.

Medicaid

Mary continues to contemplate Charles' declining health and their financial status. She realizes that in the future, nursing home care will be needed and that they can not afford the cost. She does not have sufficient income or assets to afford to pay for the care. Medicaid may be her only option to pay for nursing home care when the time comes for Charles to be placed in a nursing home.

Unlike Medicare, Medicaid is not an entitlement program. Charles will have to qualify for Medicaid. Since Medicaid is for those with low income or for the indigent, Charles can only have minimum assets. Assets can be transferred to others; however, this transfer must be made well before Charles applies for Medicaid coverage. There is a five-year look back period for transfer of assets. If assets have been transferred within five years of applying for Medicaid, Charles may be ineligible for a period of time based upon the value of the transferred assets. There are some options available to Charles, including the options available to him as a married person.

For a married couple, there are options available to provide support to the spouse. Mary, as the spouse who is not in the nursing home, referred to as the community spouse, is entitled to a monthly maintenance needs allowance. Income from the spouse qualifying for nursing home care can be used to supplement the community spouse's income so that the spouse does not become impoverished. In addition, Mary is entitled to a resource allowance that would represent a certain part of the total resources that she and Charles have. This includes certain types of annuities, cash, checking accounts, savings accounts, stocks, bonds, CDs, and the retirement plans of Charles as the nursing home eligible spouse. If eligibility is still an issue after considering Mary's monthly maintenance needs allowance and her spousal allowance, then she may have to consider spending down some of their assets so that Charles will qualify for medical assistance.

The following is a list of the type of items available for spend down:

- purchase clothing or medical equipment
- pay off debts
- prepay funeral and burial expenses
- take a vacation
- make home improvements and repairs
- upgrade the car

Further, there are assets that are specifically excluded as resources for purposes of Charles' Medicaid eligibility. Mary does not have to include any of the following items when applying for Medicaid for Charles:

- The primary residence is an excluded resource because Mary is a community spouse. If Charles was not married, the house could still be excluded as a resource if Charles intends to return to the home. However, if the equity in the home exceeds $500,000 (in Pennsylvania, may be higher in other states), whether married or not, Charles would not be eligible for medical assistance, Medicaid. Unless Mary (the community spouse) intends to continue to reside in the home, then the equity limit is not applicable. That is the situation for Mary and Charles. Therefore, the substantial home equity limit would not affect Charles' eligibility for Medicaid.

- One car is an excluded asset.

- Household goods and personal effects are excluded.

- Pension funds of the community spouse, Mary, are excluded.

- Certain qualified annuity purchases are excluded.

Even though Charles does not currently need nursing home care, now is the best time to plan. Given the look back period of five years, now may be the best time for Mary to seek advice from her attorney on asset transfer.

Long-term Care Insurance

Charles did not have long-term care insurance. Mary can, however, address long-term care insurance for herself since she now realizes just how important it is to have before it is needed.

Throughout Mary's ordeal with Charles, she has had the constant support of their son Jack, who lives nearby. Even though Mary pays for home-care for Charles while she works, Jack is able to share in the evening care of Charles. Jack also spends some weekends with Charles so that Mary has free time to relax and participate in activities outside of caring for Charles. Jack realizes how important it is that his mother takes care of her own physical and emotional health. More importantly, he has taken the initiative to help her find out all she can regarding her own potential long-term care requirements. Specifically, he wants to learn more about long-term care insurance policies, which are not only of importance to Mary but also to Jack.

Jack understands that long-term care insurance is a means to protect assets from the costs of long-term care. Without it, he sees how the care for his father is rapidly depleting his parent's assets. There may be nothing left if his mother should experience an illness. He finds that most long-term care insurance policies will pay for home-care and assisted living and cover the cost for nursing home care. The problem for Jack and Mary is being able to afford the policy and choosing a good policy.

In order to minimize the cost of long-term care insurance, it is best for Mary to purchase the insurance when she is healthy and before she gets older. She is 58 and many people start to consider the purchase of long term-care insurance in their 50s. However, it can be done earlier. Jack, for example, is only 38. However, he is a widower raising three young children. He also knows his father's diagnosis is hereditary and may be indicative of his future needs.

Long-term care insurance is a contractual agreement between an insurance company and a policy holder to pay for certain health conditions. In general, long-term care policies are sold to policyholders by insurance agents, although group policies are available as an employee benefit, through membership organizations, and from health maintenance organizations. In choosing a good policy, Jack and Mary might consider the following:

1. **Purchase sufficient coverage.** You want to get enough coverage to pay for the cost of long-term care. This can be done by considering the current cost of nursing home care and the inflationary rate in order to project the future cost. The insurance company will assist with this projection. If you fail to get adequate long-term care coverage the future cost could bankrupt your family.

2. **Purchase a home-care option or rider.** You want to make sure that your long-term care coverage provides for such care in your home. You want coverage not only while you are in a nursing home, but if you can get skilled care in the home you want that covered by your long-care insurance as well. You do not want to be financially compelled to go to a nursing home. It would be in the best interest of both Jack and Mary to add coverage for home care to help them avoid moving to a nursing home.

3. **Purchase several years of coverage.** After moving to a nursing home, Mary may want to transfer assets to Jack. As explained in the prior section on Medicaid, such transfer would result in an extended period of Medicaid ineligibility. After that extended period has passed, only then can Mary qualify for Medicaid to pay her nursing home costs (provided the assets remaining in her name do not exceed Medicaid's limits). If she employs this strategy, she will need long-term care coverage only for the years before

Medicaid coverage commences. Five years of long-term care coverage may be sufficient. A longer period may be needed if Mary does not intend to transfer any assets to become eligible for Medicaid. Long-term care insurance would serve as her private payment for the length of time she is in the nursing home as well as anytime she may have required home-care before going into the nursing home. Given the unknown length of time anyone may require long-term care in the future, many individuals purchase between three to five years of long-term care coverage. Longer terms, of course, are also available.

4. **Do not make misrepresentations or false statements in the application for coverage.** If in completing the application for insurance, Mary fails to tell the insurer about an illness or a doctor's visit, the company may refuse her coverage at the time benefits are needed. It is better to be denied a policy and be able to plan knowing that coverage is not available than to believe that coverage will be forthcoming, only to have it denied when it is most needed. This is even more important for Jack because he needs to know whether his father's diagnosis will make him as Charles' son, ineligible for long-term care insurance. Planning ahead gets answers to this question and many other important questions.

5. **Shop for the best company and best rate.** Both Jack and Mary need to make certain that the insurer is a highly rated insurance company. The coverage will not be effective if the insurer goes out of business in your time of need. In addition, rates charged by insurance companies in the long-term care field tend to vary widely. Mary and Jack have to compare different companies' rates and offering before making a final decision.

As an incentive to plan ahead, qualified long-term care insurance policies receive special tax treatment. To be qualified, policies must adhere to regulations established by the National Association of Insurance

Commissioners. The policy must offer the options of inflation protection as well as nonforfeiture protection. The latter protection allows for money back if the policy lapses. It is not required that the optional provisions are actually purchased. Some states have special tax benefits as well.

These tax advantaged, long-term care policies must offer both activities of daily living (ADL) and cognitive impairment triggers for coverage. Under the ADL trigger, benefits may begin only when beneficiary needs assistance with at least two of six ADL, which are eating, going to the bathroom, transferring, bathing, dressing, or if the individual is incontinent. In addition, a licensed healthcare practitioner must certify that the need for assistance with the ADL is reasonably expected to continue for at least 90 days. Under a cognitive impairment trigger, coverage begins when the individual has been certified to require drugs/medications supervision to protect the person from threats to health and safety due to cognitive impairment.

Premiums for qualified long-term care policies will be treated as a medical expense and will be deducted to the extent that they, along with other unreimbursed medical expenses, exceed a percentage of the insured's adjusted gross income. However, the taxpayer's age determines the maximum long-term care insurance premium that is deductible.

Staying in the Home

Studies show that most Americans, as they age, prefer to stay in their own home if they possibly can. This is not a surprise. As a result of this preference, most care, as is the case for Charles and Mary, is provided at home, by family, or by hired help. This does have many consequences, some of which may be quite unexpected.

To begin with, family members shoulder most of the responsibility of caring for elders at home. Being the primary caregiver for someone who requires assistance with activities of daily living, such as walking, eating, dressing, and going to the bathroom can be an all-consuming and exhausting task. An important consideration is the question of equity with other family members when one family member has the sole responsibility of caring for a parent or other elder relative. Should a child be compensated for the work? If the parent is living with a child, does the parent help pay for the house? If the care is taking place in the parent's home, should the child have an ownership interest in the house?

For parents with only one child, such arrangements may not be so complicated, but if the parent has more than one child, equity does become an issue. An arrangement that seems equitable today may not seem that way after a child has devoted a number of years to the parent's care. If a plan is set up that is fair for several years of care, what happens if the parent suddenly moves into a nursing home during the first year? With no planning for such eventualities, the care of a parent can foster resentment and guilt among family members.

The family care agreement, sometimes referred to as a personal service contract, has been a way to address some of these issues. It is an agreement between an elderly person and one or more persons (family member or unrelated person) to provide care, including housing if necessary for the elderly person for a specified term, which may be for life.

In the family arrangement, the agreement can cover the services provided by the family member, the fee for the service, and how that fee is paid. Another important issue that can be addressed in the family care agreement is the ownership of the family home. If the parent has to go to a nursing home, can the family home be protected from nursing home costs? In such a situation, the parent's home could be transferred to any child who resided in the home for at least two years prior to admission to the nursing home and provided care to the parent. It must be demonstrated that the care provided enabled the parent to stay at home rather than have to go to a nursing home.

State and federal government officials are slowly recognizing that home-care is much more cost-effective than long term institutional care. Depending on the state, financial or other non-financial assistance may be available for those who choose to remain in their homes despite declining capabilities.

In Pennsylvania, one such example is the Pennsylvania Department of Aging Waiver Program (PDA 60 plus Waiver Program). It is designed to reduce state expenditures by providing home and community-based services to certain individuals who would otherwise need nursing home care but who can be safely cared for at home with the supportive services provided under the program. The PDA is responsible for conducting the medical assessments, facilitating the application for services, and arranging for the delivery of the supportive services to qualified recipients on a statewide basis.

The PDA 60 plus Waiver Program provides personal care services, respite care, Older Adult Daily Living Centers, environmental modifications, transportation, specialized medical equipment and supplies, personal emergency response system, extended state plan physician services, companion services, home support extended state plan physician services, home health, home-delivered meals, and attendant care. In order to qualify for the PDA 60 plus Waiver program, the applicant must be 60 or older. They must also meet the financial restrictions applicable for non-money medical assistance as well as be medically assessed as nursing home clinically eligible.

If it is possible for the individual to be safely cared for at home at less expense than the average statewide medical assistance payment (Medicaid) for nursing home care, the applicant may choose the PDA 60 plus Waiver program rather than care in a facility. Access to the program is contingent upon the availability of a PDA 60 plus Waiver slot. Individuals 60 or older are automatically financially eligible for the program and do not have to apply if they are currently receiving medical assistance (Medicaid) or SSI benefits.

Throughout all states, public and private agencies offer a variety of home-care services that may be needed:

- healthcare in the home, either part-time or 24-hour care

- personal care services, such as cleaning, shopping, and cooking

- special services at home, such as meals programs, transportation, lawn care, and home repair

- day care centers for seniors

- financial planning and money management focused on the unique needs of elders

- programs for caretakers to take a periodic break

Assisted Living

Though staying at home is the preference for most Americans, there has been an increase of supportive housing alternatives. The options are no longer limited to an agonizing choice between staying at home and moving to a nursing home.

Assisted living facilities are one supportive housing alternative that has experienced significant growth. These facilities provide room, board, and 24 hour supervision as well as help with some of the six activities of daily living (ADL). Housing is often in small apartments where there are medical supervision and recreational options.

Assisted living facilities are not as costly as nursing home care, though the expense is significant. Where the average cost in 2009 for nursing homes in Pennsylvania is approximately $7,000, for assisted living facilities, the average cost is approximately $3,000. The cost varies depending upon the level of service provided by the facility and the specific needs of the person.

Continuing Care Retirement Communities (CCRC)

Another supportive housing alternative is the Continuing Care Retirement Communities. These communities offer a blend of housing complex, activity center, and health care services. They can consist of independent living, assisted living, and nursing care as well as other programs and activities. Some offer specialized Alzheimer's memory care units and programs.

There are various types of CCRCs. They differ in the nature of services included or that are optional, the payment structure, the refundability (or non-refundability) of the entrance fee, as well as the physical design features of the accommodations. The three major areas that can be used to assist in defining the types of CCRCs are as follows:

Services (other than healthcare/nursing care)

Most CCRCs offer a series of services or programs that are either included within the monthly fees or may be separately purchased or accessed on-site for an additional fee. Examples include the following:

- Meals - This changed over time to reflect preference for more flexibility. Today, most CCRCs either include a meal per day or some number of meals per month (such as 15 to 20) or offer a monthly dining allowance which can be used whenever the resident chooses.

- Housekeeping - weekly, bi-weekly, monthly, or as needed

- Transportation - on a scheduled basis to local shopping and other sites. Transportation to personal appointments and medical services may be offered as needed for an additional fee.

- Activities - recreational options including fitness programs, aquatics, arts, crafts

- Other - emergency response or emergency call

Healthcare Options

CCRCs can offer independent living, assisted living, and nursing care. Many offer all three levels of care or services, though there are some that do not include nursing care as part of the covered continuum or which offer nursing care at a separate location. There are three primary types of healthcare options:

The **first type** provides an individual with the ability to move from independent living to assisted living or nursing care without any significant change in their monthly payment. For example, if a resident was paying $3,000 for a one-bedroom apartment but now requires round the clock skilled nursing care in this type of community, the monthly fee would remain at $3,000 with some additional charge for three meals per day that are required by long-term care regulation. This first type of community tends to have higher entrance fees and higher monthly fees than the second and third types of communities.

The **second type** is sometimes referred to as modified fee-for-service communities. There are various forms of these communities, but essential life care is not offered. The resident does not have to pay the full cost of the higher levels of care, either because they receive a discount on the per diem or monthly costs for the higher levels of care (i.e. assisted living and nursing care) or receive an agreed upon number of days within the higher care levels, without additional charge to their independent living unit monthly fee.

The **third type** is frequently referred to as fee-for-service communities. The monthly fee in particular (but also entrance fees) tends to be lower than the fee at other types of communities. The reason for this is that there is no insurance component. If independent living residents require assisted living or nursing care, they can access that care but will be charged the full cost of the care. There is no discount or free days. While the advantage of the first type is that they offer residents and families the ability to define and pre-plan the expenditures that will be made for current and future care, these communities, of course, tend to be more expensive. The third type recognizes that not all residents will require higher levels of care; therefore, the resident is only charged for the actual care that is received.

Payment Options

Another key distinguishing characteristic of CCRCs is the refundability of the entrance fee. The four basic types of entrance fee approaches are as follows:

Non-refundable   The entrance fee is non-refundable in the event of the resident's death. Non-refundable entrance fees are generally lower than the remainder of the entrance fee options described below.

Amortized An amortized entrance fee generally offers the resident or the resident's estate the ability to recoup a portion of the entrance fee paid during an agreed upon period.

Refundable The term refundable entrance fee is typically used to describe an entrance fee that offers the resident or the resident's estate the ability to always obtain a specific refund amount – as a minimum.

Equity Though less common, it is another payment option for some CCRCs. The equity approach represents entrance fee refund plans that offer the resident or the resident's estate the ability to obtain a refund that reflects a portion of the appreciation of the resident's living unit or apartment.

Guardianship

When Eve's husband Bob died, she became extremely depressed and, for a few days, had to be institutionalized. Afterwards, she no longer cared about their business of breeding show dogs. Within three years of Bob's death, the business had to be dissolved and the remaining dogs given to one of Bob's favorite charities consistent with the terms of the established dissolution plan. Eve eventually relinquished all of her board positions with local and national charities and sold the home that she and Bob had shared and in which they reared their only child Julia. She secluded herself in their remote lakeside cabin away from all her friends and family. Her daughter was the only one with whom she did spend some time. She did not trust Julia's husband, who seemed to be more interested in Julia's wealth than in Julia.

Just before Bob's death, Eve had updated her estate plan documents. In her general power of attorney for handling her finances and business affairs, she named as her agent her financial advisor and close personal friend Mary. Eve's daughter Julia serves as her agent under her healthcare power of attorney and surrogate under her living will. Even though Julia does not want money left to her by her mother to be placed in a trust, it still remains that way, to Julia's husband's dismay.

During her visits, Julia has growing concerns regarding her mother's sanity. Eve eats very little and seldom ventures out of the cabin now. She refuses to address her depression and only expresses to her daughter that she wants to be left alone to join Bob, so Julia wants to pursue guardianship of her mother.

It is important to have both a healthcare power of attorney and general power of attorney. As discussed in chapters 5 and 6, both of these documents allow Eve to appoint a person to act as her agent if she becomes incapacitated or needs someone to act on her behalf. In Eve's case, that would be Mary to handle financial and other business affairs and Julia to handle medical affairs. It is also important that her power of attorney includes nominations for guardian of the estate and guardian of the person in the event a guardianship proceeding is ever filed. The nominees for guardian of the estate and guardian of the person need not be the same person. In Eve's power of attorney, she designated Mary (not Julia) to serve as guardian. If Eve did not have a power of attorney or it did not address guardianship, any qualified individual, a corporate fiduciary, a nonprofit corporation, a guardian support agency, or a county agency, could be appointed by the court to serve as Eve's guardian. The court has discretion to appoint a guardian who will best serve her interests, and the court's decision will not be reversed absent abuse of discretion.

Eve has made it clear that she knows exactly what she is doing and can make her own decisions. Throughout her life, she has been a strong, independent, and successful business woman. Her decision to now lead a private and solitary life is, in her opinion, her prerogative, and she refuses to let anyone deter her.

In recent times, Eve has become increasingly agitated with Julia's and Mary's interference. For example, Julia has advised Eve's doctors that Eve needs a psychiatric evaluation and needs to be treated for severe depression. Further, Mary has questioned Eve's decision to transfer significant assets within her control to anyone that can communicate with her dead husband. As a result, Eve has terminated her powers of attorney and thus revoked any authority for Julia and Mary to act on her behalf. She has also fired Mary as her financial advisor.

Julia's attorney for the guardianship proceedings explains the law and their likelihood of success. Her attorney advises that under the law, an incapacitated person means an adult whose ability to receive and evaluate information effectively and communicate decisions in any way is impaired to a significant extent that she is partially or totally unable to manage her financial resources or to meet essential requirements for her physical health and safety. This means the focus is on the existence and extent of Eve's impairment. The essential inquiry under current law is the actual capacity of Eve to understand and make decisions. However, only if it is determined that Eve needs guardianship services will the courts in Pennsylvania actually adjudicate Eve as incapacitated. The courts consider such factors as the availability of family, friends, and other supports to assist Eve in making decisions and in light of the existence, if any, of advance directives such as general powers of attorney or trusts. Even though Eve has terminated her power of attorney, most of her assets are held and administered under trusts set up by Bob. This may alleviate the need for guardianship service of Eve's estate and thus the determination of full incapacity will not be found. If Eve is already being sufficiently cared for by family, friends, or a substantial "circle of support," then there is no need to make a finding on incapacity since there is no need for guardianship services.

The attorney further explains to Julia that all of this means that Eve may be incapacitated by all accounts of her physicians. However, she will only be declared incapacitated by the courts if there is no one or no arrangement in place to help Eve in her current state or condition. With that being said, Julia's attorney proceeds to explain Julia's options.

Julia could pursue a plenary (very broad) guardianship or limited guardianship. The limited guardian is to allow an incapacitated person to retain as much liberty and personal autonomy as possible. It is a more flexible alternative, appropriate if a court finds that Eve is only partially incapacitated and in need of limited guardianship services of the person or estate or both. The appointed guardian may only exercise powers consistent with the court's findings of limitations. Except in those specific areas over which the guardian is given authority, the partially incapacitated person retains all other legal rights.

If the court were to find that Eve is partially incapacitated and in need of guardianship services, the powers granted to the limited guardian of the person are to be tailored to be consistent with the court's findings as to Eve's limitations and may include the following:

1. general care, maintenance, and custody of Eve

2. deciding where Eve should live

3. assuring that Eve receives psychological services, as appropriate

4. assisting Eve to regain maximum self-reliance and independence

5. providing required consents and approvals on Eve's behalf

The powers of a limited guardian of the estate, (as opposed to the person) should also be consistent with the court's findings, if any, as to Eve's limitations. The court's order must specify the portion of Eve's assets or income over which the guardian is assigned powers and duties. In those limited areas over which the guardian has authority, Eve, if determined by the court to be a partially incapacitated person, would then lack the capacity to form contracts, make gifts, or execute other written instruments. However, Eve retains legal title to all of her property and may have testamentary capacity to execute a valid will or change an existing one.

Plenary guardianship results if Eve is found to be totally incapacitated and in need of full guardianship services. If Eve is in the care of a plenary guardian, she lacks the capacity to form contracts, make gifts, or execute other written instruments.

Eve is presumed mentally competent, and the burden is on Julia to prove her mother's incapacity by clear and convincing evidence. This should include proof that Eve can not correctly evaluate information and that she can not appropriately communicate decisions. Her evaluation and communication skills are impaired. Further, as a result of this impairment, Eve is either partially or totally unable to manage her financial resources or provide for her physical health and safety. Finally, Julia has to establish that the only way to address her mother's situation is with guardianship services.

No presumption of incapacity can be raised based on Eve's prior institutionalization. Julia must present testimony from individuals qualified by training and experience to evaluate the type of incapacity alleged. That testimony must establish the nature and extent of Eve's incapacities and disabilities, and Eve's mental, emotional, and physical condition, as well as her adaptive behavior and social skills.

Julia must also present evidence regarding the following:

1. the services providing for Eve's physical health and safety

2. the steps being taken to manage Eve's financial resources

3. the help Eve is receiving to develop or regain her abilities

4. the types of assistance Eve needs

5. the reasons why less restrictive alternatives are insufficient

6. the probability that the extent of Eve's incapacities will lessen or change

Eve has the right to cross-examine witnesses testifying as to her incapacity.

If the court determines that Eve is incapacitated and requires guardianship services, it is not predetermined that the guardian will be the person who instituted guardianship proceedings. In this case, Julia instituted guardianship proceedings. It is within the court's discretion to select a guardian. Eve has not provided for her preference regarding a guardian since she terminated her prior power of attorney that named Mary. Eve did not execute a new power of attorney.

The duties and responsibilities of a person's guardian are established by law. The guardian must assert Eve's rights and best interests. In exercising this duty, the guardian must respect Eve's expressed wishes and preferences to the greatest possible extent. Where appropriate, the guardian assures and contributes to the developing of a plan of support services to meet Eve's needs. The guardian is also required to encourage Eve to participate - to the maximum extent possible - in all decisions that affect her. Eve must also be encouraged to act on her own behalf as much as she is able and to develop or regain her capacity to manage her affairs.

Summary

The information throughout this chapter as well as the other chapters will be of benefit to you and your family today, tomorrow, and for generations. Share what you have learned with others so that we have a movement to action for all those individuals who have been waiting before they take the necessary estate planning steps. Maybe your encouragement and sharing this book with friends and family will answer the question, "What are you waiting for?"

Appendix

WORKSHEET
FAMILY INFORMATION

Date: _____

ALL THE INFORMATION PROVIDED IN THIS FORM SHALL REMAIN CONFIDENTIAL CLIENT INFORMATION. IT SHALL NOT BE RELEASED, SHARED, OR DISCUSSED WITH ANY OTHER PARTY WITHOUT THE EXPRESSED WRITTEN CONSENT OF THE CLIENT.

I. GENERAL INFORMATION: (for you and spouse)

NAME and SOCIAL SECURITY NO.	DATE OF BIRTH	U.S. CITIZEN (Yes or No)

ADDRESS:
TOWNSHIP/BOROUGH/COUNTY:

EMAIL:
PHONE NUMBERS: Home:
                                      Work:

PRIOR MARRIAGES:

CLIENT NAME:	PRIOR SPOUSE NAME	DATE OF DEATH OR DIVORCE

CHILDREN:

NAME (WHICH MARRIAGE)	AGE, DATE OF BIRTH	ADDRESS	MARITAL STATUS/NO. OF CHILDREN

OCCUPATION:

NAME	OCCUPATION	EMPLOYER	ADDRESS/ PHONE NO.

PROFESSIONAL ADVISORS:

	NAME	ADDRESS	PHONE NUMBER
Attorneys			
Accountants			
Insurance Agents			
Financial Advisors			

II. BENEFICIARY(IES)
A. PRIMARY BENEFICIARY(IES)

	NAME	RELATIONSHIP	ADDRESS
Primary Beneficiary(ies)			
Property to be received			
Primary Beneficiary(ies)			
Property to be received			
Primary Beneficiary(ies)			
Property to be received			

B. SECONDARY BENEFICIARY(IES): (Inherit in the event your primary beneficiary(ies) does not survive you)

	NAME	RELATIONSHIP	ADDRESS
Secondary Beneficiary(ies)			
Property to be received			
Secondary Beneficiary(ies)			
Property to be received			
Secondary Beneficiary(ies)			
Property to be received			

III. FIDUCIARIES (for last will & testament)

List in order of preference the persons and/or institution (such as a bank or trust company) you wish to name as your executor. Name at least two (primary and alternate) if you do not name a bank. For married clients, husband is usually named first for wife, and wife is usually named first as executor for husband, and each would then name someone else as an alternate.

As husband, I desire to name my wife as my executor. _____ Yes _____ No
As wife, I desire to name my husband as my executor. _____ Yes _____ No

1. **Executor** (sometimes called "personal representative") the person(s) who will be responsible for administering your estate:

	NAME	ADDRESS	RELATIONSHIP TO YOU
Primary			
Alternate			

2. **Guardian** (the person who will care for minor - under the age of 18 - children in the event of the death of both spouses):

	NAME	ADDRESS	RELATIONSHIP TO YOU
Primary			
Alternate			

3. **Custodian Under the Uniform Transfers to Minors Act** (the person who will be responsible for any property left to minor children until they reach the age of majority:

	NAME	ADDRESS	RELATIONSHIP TO YOU
Primary			
Alternate			

4. **Trustee of Trusts You Create in Your Will** (the person(s) and/or bank you wish to name as trustee for minor children or others.)

	NAME	ADDRESS	RELATIONSHIP TO YOU
Primary			
Alternate			

5. **Who Will Manage Your Revocable Living Trust?** (Original Trustee(s): You will be the initial trustee(s) unless you designate otherwise. Successor Trustees): At your death or disability, your backups will manage your trust. Your backup trustee can be your adult children, financial advisor, trusted friend, bank and/or a trust company. If you select an individual, you should name a second choice in case your first is unable to serve.)

	NAME	ADDRESS	RELATIONSHIP TO YOU
Primary			
Alternate			

B. General Power of Attorney: (Provide this information only if you wish to have a general power of attorney prepared)

1. **Agent** (the person(s) who will handle your financial affairs in the event you become disabled):

   (a) **Yourself:**

	NAME	ADDRESS	RELATIONSHIP TO YOU
Primary			
Alternate			

   (b) **Your Spouse:**

	NAME	ADDRESS	RELATIONSHIP TO YOU
Primary			
Alternate			

2. **Real Estate Owned**

ADDRESS OF PROPERTY	NAME(S) IN WHICH HELD	DEED DATE	DEED REFERENCE (LIBER AND FOLIO AT TOP OF DOCUMENT)

C. Medical Power of Attorney: (Please provide this information only if you wish to have a medical power of attorney prepared)

1. **Agent** (the person(s) who will make medical decisions on your behalf, regarding your care, in the event you become disabled and cannot make such decisions for yourself):

(a) **Yourself:**

	NAME	ADDRESS	RELATIONSHIP TO YOU
Primary			
Alternate			

(b) **Your Spouse:**

	NAME	ADDRESS	RELATIONSHIP TO YOU
Primary			
Alternate			

D. Military Service: (Please provide this information regarding military service applicable to you or your spouse. Include branch, years of service and current status)

E. Living Will

Do you wish to have a living will?

F. Special Needs/Disability

Does any beneficiary have any special needs?

G. Family Pets

Are you interested in any special provision for the care of a family pet?

IV. LIST OF ASSETS AND LIABILITIES ESTATE ASSET SUMMARY PAGE

For each type of asset held by you and your spouse, indicate the total value by title (sole title in your name, joint with spouse and sole title in spouse's name). The following pages are included to detail each asset and liability.

ASSET	CLIENT'S SOLE NAME	JOINT	SPOUSE'S SOLE NAME
Personal Residence (Today's Market Value)			
Second Home (Today's Market Value)			
Total of Other Real Estate (Today's Market Value)			
Cash, Bank Accounts, Money Market Funds & CDs			
Stocks & Mutual Funds			
Bonds, Bond Funds & Treasury Bills			
Household Furnishings and Personal Assets			
Jewelry			
Automobiles			
Retirement Assets (IRA'S, 401(k), 403(b) & Pension Death Benefits			
Profit-Sharing Plan			
Closely-Held Businesses and/or Farms			
Powers of Appointment			
Interest in Estates and Trusts			
Life Insurance (Face Value)			
Annuities			
TOTAL ASSETS			

Appendix: Worksheet - Family Information

155

Index

STOP! What Are You Waiting For?
Your Step-By-Step Guide to Estate Planning
Order Form

Internet Orders:	www.ythlaw.com
Fax Orders:	Complete this form and fax to 1(215) 321-1999
Mail Orders:	Second Wind Press, P.O. Box 407
	Washington Crossing, PA 18977, USA

Please contact me:

☐ I am interested in having the author make an appearance for a speaking engagement

☐ I would like to have a book signing for the author

Please send more **FREE** information on:

☐ Other Books, ☐ Speaking/Seminars, ☐ Mailing Lists, ☐ Consulting

Name: _____
       First   Last   Middle

Address: _____

City: _____ State: _____ Zip: ____ - ____

Telephone: ( ) _____ Email Address: _____

Please send _____ copies of Stop! What Are You Waiting For? Your Step-By-Step Guide to Estate Planning at \$30.44 each, total includes the book, shipping and sales tax. (Deduct \$1.80 per book for books delivered outside of Pennsylvania.)

Payment: ☐ Check, ☐ Credit Card:

Make Checks Payable to: Yvette E. Taylor-Hachoose, LLC

☐ Visa, ☐ MasterCard, ☐ AMEX ☐ Discover

Card Number: _____

Name on Card: _____ Exp. Date: ____ / ____

See http://www.buckscountyattorney.blogspot.com
Percentage of net proceeds donated to the charity www.lifegivingwater.org